Jesus the Healer

A Testimony of Healing and Conversion

Shirley Keogh

*I dedicate this work to the
Holy Family of Nazareth*

Endorsements

"It has often been said that 'one healing is worth a thousand sermons'. This is certainly true in the case of Shirley Keogh's graphic account of her spiritually inspired healing of the wounds of a childhood trauma following the divorce of her parents. We often hear of the positive aspects of the 'law of unintended consequences' but rarely of the negative effects – especially those of the traumas experienced by young children when parents separate.

In this frank and honest memoir, Shirley details the painful, emotional scars she experienced when as a 12 year old child she was cut off, not only from her father, but also from her younger brother. In a beautifully crafted fashion, she describes the impact that the separation had on her but more importantly how her journey towards the healing of her wound led her into her present vocation – to be a voice and a source of healing for others, who through no fault of their own, have had to travel a similar path.

Using a diary-journaling technique she details the steps by which she was led to surrender her life and her problems to the Lord. It was revealed to her that 'by His stripes' we are healed, as the Lord led her to a place of hope and healing. She now had the courage to share her story in the hope that her experiences may help society to think again about the widespread (and growing) availability of divorce and parental separation. She makes a heartfelt plea for the real victims - the children.

As a wife and mother she realises that the deepest healing is that of a broken heart and a bruised spirit. As a committed Christian, Shirley explains that in the Catholic tradition healing is more likely to come in a gradual way. For many people brought up in a world where everything is instant and immediate, she points out that we can learn so many valuable lessons about life in the waiting period – things that we can easily miss in more dramatic and instantaneous stories of healing.

Shirley is living proof that when we surrender our lives to the Lord He can mysteriously open doors that we didn't even know existed. I am very pleased to recommend her book and pray that it will provide readers with as much encouragement and hope as it has given me."

~Fr Benny McHale

"Shirley Keogh has taken a courageous gamble in laying her spiritual heart so bare. I believe it has paid off. This is a warm, brave and hospitable book where searchers and believers can find refreshment, encouragement and rest. Shirley has placed all the fruits of her own search and ever-deepening faith on this excellent table. I recommend it with enthusiasm and confidence and I pray it has a wonderful effect in its readers' lives."

~Rev. Brendan Kilcoyne, PP Athenry

"In this beautiful book of meditations, stories, Scriptural teachings and more, Shirley Keogh has written what will doubtless be a great blessing for the faithful who read it. Her writing is inspiring, edifying, and bears great witness to the power of Christ in our lives. May all who open these pages be likewise encouraged to grow into ever deeper union with Our Lord and allow Him to transform their lives!"

~Daniel S D O'Connor

Renowned Theologian, author of '*The Crown of Sanctity - On the Revelations of Jesus to Luisa Piccarreta*' and contributor to www.Countdowntothekingdom.com.

Acknowledgements

Special thanks to my beloved husband for all his support during the writing of this book.

I wish to give my special love and appreciation to my parents who instilled in me a love for learning and have encouraged and supported me over the years with my education, work and family.

A special word of love and gratitude to my brother for his kindness, thoughtfulness and good humour.

Heartfelt thanks also to all my spiritual friends and 'helpers' along the way who have guided me along this journey, especially the holy parishioner from Athenry and our holy priests in St. Mary's Church, Athenry: Fr Benny, who encouraged me to go the Medjugorje and the Holy Land, Fr Brendan, for encouraging me to write a presentation of my story and Fr Jerald for his wonderful teaching of the Catholic Catechism.

About the Author

The author and her husband live with their four children in a rural setting in County Galway, Ireland. Shirley has written about her miraculous journey to gradual healing from a traumatic break-up of the family unit in childhood when she was separated from her younger brother.

She introduces us to this healing journey by outlining: her early family life, meeting her future husband during the college years, her professional career in the corporate world, starting a family and becoming a primary school teacher in her forties.

She has set out the key events which have shaped the healing process: the local holy woman who reached out to help her, Christian counselling in Esker, the healing mission in Clonfert, and pilgrimages to Medjugorje and the Holy Land. The wonderful healing she experienced led her to write her inspirations in a diary format. Thus began a realisation that she was now being called by Jesus and Mary to help others who are suffering from childhood trauma.

To this end, the author has availed of many opportunities to pass on the message of the healing love of Jesus and Mary in her day to day life, in her family, at work or chance meetings socially as directed through prayer and guidance from heaven.

In the run up to the divorce referendum in Ireland in May 2019, the author wrote a letter to 'The Irish Catholic' newspaper, which was published, warning people of the problems associated with divorce, and she also recorded a testimony for GRIPT Media on the same subject.

She offers up her prayers and sufferings in advance for the prayer intentions of all readers of this book and wishes them all the blessings that a healed life in Jesus brings.

'And now these three remain: faith, hope and love. But the greatest of these is love.' **1 Corinthians 13:13.**[1]

' *I am the way, the truth, and the life, no one comes to the Father except by me.'* **John 14:6.**[1]

Contents

Chapter One

Introduction

'Thank you Jesus and Mary for helping to write my story.'

I was born in the Rotunda Hospital, Dublin in December 1968, the eldest of two children; the same month the first humans were to travel to and orbit the moon on the spacecraft Apollo 8.

I spent the first twelve years of my life living in Dublin's inner city close to the convent of the Sisters of Charity, Manor Street, where I attended St Joseph's primary school. The family break up happened when I was twelve years old and my brother was eight years old. My brother lived with our dad in the family home while my mother and I lived in rented accommodation in Drumcondra for two years before moving to England. My parents were eventually divorced.

I would consider myself extremely blessed in my life despite and because of the sufferings I went through following the break-down of the family unit.

You may ask why I am writing this. Actually, the reason is very simple, I would like to help others who may be suffering from a childhood trauma as I was helped when I said 'yes' to Jesus.

I would also add that what follows might help anyone who needs to recover 'fully' and 'completely' from any deep-seated emotional or mental wound. It doesn't matter what you have done or been through, Jesus is waiting for you at the door to take your first step and he will welcome you with open arms.

The story is written in the format of a diary because it will show the reader how our relationship with Jesus is an ongoing process of conversion and is full of opportunities to get to know Him better. If you have fallen away from the Church, it is of no consequence. This testimony will show you how 'as' I opened my heart to Jesus bit by bit, I was healed from the pain of my past.

You may even live a good life, have a good job, be financially secure etc. I had all these things. But material things are transient and can be lost in a heartbeat. What's left, if you lose this material security, if you have no faith foundations, if you have no trust in the Lord only yourself and you find you haven't all the answers but feel you somehow must find a solution to your problems? In my situation as a child, I felt somewhat guilty for the breakdown of my parents' marriage.

The diary dates in Chapter two detail my journey to conversion and are interspersed with my prayers to and 'inspirations' from Jesus and my own experiences of Him working in my everyday life.

December 1968

My mum was in her early twenties when she had me and my father was not present at the birth. They had been married earlier that year. At that time in his life he was 'a bit fond of the drink' though he thankfully gave it up for good a few years later. We lived within walking distance from Dublin city centre for the first six months of my life and it was near the hospital where my parents first met and worked. However the marriage was quite turbulent and my mother left my father the first time when I was six months old and went to stay with her sister in England. My dad travelled over to England to persuade her to come home, which she did.

We lived with Dad's parents, for a while after that. They were a lovely couple – Pauline and John. I remember, years later, John hiding a bar of chocolate in a press one day. He called me over with a gesture from his finger and pointed to the press. When he opened the door of the press (cupboard) there was a lovely purple wrapped bar of Dairy Milk chocolate on the shelf. I thought I'd died and gone to heaven.

A bar of dairy milk would be a real treat back in the early seventies.

My first memory of my little brother Tom was when he was brought home from the hospital. He had the remnants of the umbilical cord still attached to his little body. He was born on August 22, 1973. I was three and half years old.

My parents worked as nurses in St Brendan's Hospital for the psychiatrically ill in Grangegorman, though my mother stayed at home when we were small. It is now a Dublin Institute of Technology. The landscape has changed a lot since we were carefree children playing on the grounds of the hospital. We thought we were fortunate to have a huge green area with fields and gardens to play in within a short distance walk from Dublin City centre. Kids from the local streets used to come and play there. There didn't seem to be any parents around when we were playing. Perhaps there was less fear of anything happening to children back then even though you could often see psychiatric patients who were on medication walking up and down the Villas when we were small. It was apparent even to a child that the patients didn't look quite right. They generally had a faraway look in their eyes, shirt-tails hanging out, usually very dishevelled looking. It was hard not to stare. I'm sure we were told by our parents not to pay any heed to them and to look straight ahead…

Growing up in the 1970s

Moore Street in the 1970s was a far cry from what it is today. I distinctly remember tough but healthy, robust-looking women selling oranges and apples 'foive for fifty' on that narrow street off Henry street on the north side of the city. It was hard to ignore them as they shouted 'apples and oranges – foive for fifty. Come and buy the lovely juicy oranges .' brown bags already opened and waiting to be filled. Arnotts and Cleary's were the two main stores on the North side of the river Liffey in town. My mother would always stop off in the coffee shop in Arnott's during a day out shopping. It's one of my fond memories of town – Arnott's café, and a welcome reprieve from window shopping!

Quite a few years later, the other well-known store, Cleary's, would be the main meeting point for meeting friends and dates. We would arrange to meet under Cleary's clock at a certain time. There were no mobile phones at that time to let someone know if you were going to be late! Years later we would all marvel at the new invention of the mobile phone. Who would have known that it would be central to Irish social life in years to come.

School and College Life

I would say I was quite hardworking at school. On account of the family break up I attended three different secondary schools, the first one in St Joseph's, Stanhope Street, where I spent the first two years. This was followed by Goring Catholic High school in Sussex in England where I studied for and obtained nine 'O' Levels in 1985. ('O' Levels comparatively speaking are equivalent to the year in between the Junior Certificate and the Leaving certificate). After living for two years in England my mum and I returned to Ireland, and I subsequently applied for and got a place in Dominican Convent secondary school in Griffith Avenue. I received an honours Leaving certificate and went on to study for a primary degree in Social Science at UCD. I graduated in 1990. By this time, I had an idea of what I wanted to do in terms of a career. I was attracted to the Personnel Management option in the Masters of Business Studies programme and so I applied for that. I obtained a Master's degree in Business Studies, which I attained with honours in 1991.

Meeting my Soulmate

It was towards the end of my college years that I met Eamon. If ever there was a story of 'it was meant to be' this is it! I met him at my friend's twenty first birthday party. We spotted each other across a crowded room and eventually towards the end of the night we got talking. We clicked straight away. We found out a number of months later that we could have met a year earlier at a mutual friend's birthday party. The friend had invited me, but I wasn't able to come as I was working in my part-time job that evening. So I didn't meet him then! It would be another year before I met my future husband.

We married in Corpus Christi Church in Drumcondra in 1996. I distinctly remember feeling very happy in the Church and in the church grounds afterwards when there were just the two of us having our photos taken. It was a beautiful, heavenly, cloudless day in September..

Early Career

When I left college, I secured employment in the Personnel Department of a Medical Devices company in Tullamore. This was exactly the type of work I wanted to do, so I was very happy and enthusiastic and wanted to do well. Eamon is from Galway. Therefore, I had to go a bit further to finally settle with him in his home place! So my next job was with an insurance company in Galway. I had greater responsibility in this position and had to help the management with pay issues and the setting up of a staff forum.

At this stage, I was still ambitious to go further in my career and I could see that there were no opportunities for advancement in this firm. I saw a position advertised for a Human Resources Manager in an Engineering company in Tuam. I applied for it and had two interviews before being offered the position. I was one of the senior managers in this company, so there was international travel involved as the parent company was located in San Diego, California and there were other subsidiaries in England and France. It was to be my last corporate role. Eamon meanwhile qualified as a Quantity Surveyor and was doing well in his job in a manufacturing company. He became successful in later building projects. We were doing well financially and the icing on the cake was the news that we were expecting our first child. We decided that we could afford for me to stay at home to mind the baby. So I never returned to corporate life after that.

Family Life

Though it was quite an adjustment to stay at home with a small baby, it was such a happy time and I found I settled into a good daily routine. By the time six months had passed, I had forgotten all about my previous life as a high-flying business person! I met with other mothers regularly and later took up hobbies that I hadn't been able to do when I was working full time, such as learning how to play the piano and gardening. We had three more healthy children, thank God, our last being born in July 2008.

The Great Recession

The subprime mortgage crisis in 2006 signalled the beginning of the Great Recession.[2] By 2008 the effects were being felt in Ireland as the housing bubble burst. I remember thinking it was very strange when a person receiving social welfare payments could potentially get one hundred percent mortgage for a second property abroad. Something had to be wrong. At this stage, Eamon had his own building company and had people working for him. There was a point whereby if we had not bought our next piece of land, we would have escaped the downturn unscathed financially. However, Eamon had loyal workmen who he wanted to keep on board and so he purchased a further plot of land at a very high price to keep the lads working. This decision ultimately sank the company. Funnily enough, I remember I was with Eamon when he made the call to buy the land and I had a bad feeling about it.

Little did we know how that decision would impact our lives forever. But as they say, every cloud has a silver lining.

Going Back to Work

The loss of the business hit Eamon hard as he had worked so diligently to build it up. Meanwhile, I became more prayerful and always made sure we went to Mass on Sundays but I hadn't invited Jesus deeply into my life at that time.

When our youngest child was two years old, I made a decision to retrain as a primary school teacher. After having my own, I knew I would love working with children. It was very tough as I had been out of formal education for a long time and in fact, it had been twenty five years since I had looked at an Irish book and I knew the standard of Irish had to be high for teaching. I started off doing Irish grinds with a former Principal for six months in order to ensure I passed the interview for Hibernia College. (At that time it was an intense eighteen month post-graduate course to qualify as a primary school teacher.)

I got through the training which I can honestly say was tougher than studying for my master's degree. Thankfully teaching turned out to be the one job, during the recession, that provided lots of substitute teaching work if you were eager, hardworking and available every morning for calls from schools where teachers rang in sick. This would later develop into short term contracts, thus building a relationship with a particular school. I remember one day I had decided to give money to a specific charity and I prayed to God that He would help me to get work the following week. As soon as I came out of the post office, I got a call from a school in Ballinasloe offering me work not just for the week but for the month. Praise God!

Nevertheless, the sheer grind of going from school to school after several years took its toll and I started feeling the same insecurities I had felt as a child creeping up on me. I was beginning to doubt if I would ever get a secure permanent job again and if we would every recover from our debt situation. This feeling was compounded by the fact that Eamon was embarking on a new and risky business venture which would take him away from home leaving me to take care of the family and all their extra-curricular activities. Eventually in 2017 after much prayer, especially through the intercession of Padre Pio and the grace of God, I got a permanent teaching job in a school thirty minutes' drive from our home.

Inspired by Jesus

I was so grateful that things had worked out for me professionally and thanked St Pio and the Lord profusely. I knew that more would be expected of me. The following year (2018) I felt inspired by Jesus to start writing a diary about my faith journey to help others who might be suffering from childhood trauma. I sensed that this was one of the ways I could love my neighbour.

As the second of the Ten Commandments tells us *'Love thy neighbour as thyself.'* **Matthew 22:39** [1] In fact if everyone kept the first two commandments: 1. Love God (no false Gods), e.g. celebrity, money, image etc. and 2. Love thy neighbour - the remaining eight commandments would be easier to obey.

Chapter Two

The Beginning of My Diary

15th February 2018

Prayer

'Dear Jesus, I am here for you. Use me as an instrument of your love for humanity.'

As I pray these words, I feel a beautiful pressure on my head. It is heavier than a breeze and lighter than a hand. I experience this sensation sometimes in the Church or at adoration. At other times it could be in the sitting room or some other place. It is comforting and assures me I am doing what Jesus wants or that He just wants to comfort me. Jesus inspires me to write the following:

Jesus

'It is my Will that you tell the world I wish to communicate my love for them. I wish to give mankind the wonderful message that they can be saved. This salvation for you has been purchased by me on the cross. All of heaven is here to help you. Pray the rosary every day to keep your families together. Call on us to help you in all difficulties at every moment in the day.'

Recalling a difficult classroom situation

Prayer

'Dear Jesus, Mary and Joseph and all the angels and saints in heaven. Please help me now.'

I remember the first time I said this prayer from the heart; I was in a difficult classroom situation where everything was going wrong. I had just been to the photocopier with a sixth class pupil where I was photocopying some sheets about St Francis of Assisi for religion later that day. No matter what we did, the copies didn't come out right. They were either upside down at the back or I zoomed in too much when I was photocopying the pages. The sixth class pupil who was with me happens to be exceptionally bright and observant. She noticed how they were all 'messed up' as she put it herself. I had to return to class with the 'messed up' photocopies and there they sat on the front of my desk which is adjacent to where the student sits.

Just then another more difficult problem surfaced and this is when I said the prayer above from the heart and in desperation. A few seconds later and simultaneously, both myself and the sixth class girl noticed that the photocopies were in perfect order with no errors. We both expressed shock and joy and the same time. She said 'but they were all messed up

Miss'. 'They were!' I said. Then I told her about the prayer I had just said. She was very thoughtful for a time after that. Praise God! I subsequently gave this prayer to my children at home. My young son told me that he said the prayer on the pitch when a hurling match was going badly for him and very soon after he scored two goals for his team. God will help us in all our struggles if we ask him. **Matthew 7:8** – *'Ask and it will be given to you; seek and you will find; knock and the door will be opened to you.'* [1]

19th February 2018

Prayer

'Dear Jesus, thank you for getting me out of bed this morning to work for you. I am listening.'

Jesus

'In the beginning, there was light. Man sinned and destroyed the light. My creation ate the forbidden fruit and all humanity has paid the price. To you doubters of my existence, I am the living bread. In a similar way to how your body changes bread and water into flesh, blood and bone, I Jesus am transformed into life-giving body and blood for you at the consecration of the Mass. I the Holy One died for all your sins so that you may have life and life in all its fullness. You are

mortal and therefore forget me easily due to the pull of the world and the needs of the flesh.

These days there is a huge pull from the workplace, drawing people away from their families. I desire that you spend more time with your families and love them. Love cures all. Some of you have come from broken families and are close to me. I am helping you correct the mistakes of your past. Love your neighbour as yourself and keep my commands. Pray for those who do not love me and adore me.'

Prayer

'I love you Jesus with all my heart. Use me to save souls. Amen.'

3rd March 2018

Today I am finally feeling better after a week and a half of having the flu. It's been a while since I felt so ill and lacking in energy. The illness has made me realise that everything doesn't depend on me.

As I write this I am sitting in our sitting room with my husband and our eldest son. It's really lovely to have them. These are 'pet' days. My husband is waiting to start up building again and my son is studying for his leaving cert. My daughter is in fifth year and she has brought a cake that we bought while out shopping earlier, to Granny and Grandad's. Our two younger boys and our Spanish student are in Grandad's at the moment. Storm Emma which has rocked the country has finally abated. The white wintry landscape still lingers though it is now the 3rd March and there are lots of snowmen still standing firm in gardens around the country.

I am very aware of my mortality after having a nasty illness. Praise God that I am able to pray again. Not being able to pray and do my adoration was as upsetting as feeling ill.

17th September 2018

I felt strongly prompted by Jesus to get up and write this morning about Pope's Francis's visit to Ireland. I haven't much time as the children will be up soon to get ready for school. Time surely does go very fast when children get older. We are at the taxi service stage.

Recalling Pope Francis's Visit to Ireland 25th and 26th August 2018

When the tickets were first advertised for the Pope's visit to Ireland, I recalled the occasion when Pope John Paul II came to visit Ireland in 1979 in the Phoenix Park in Dublin. I travelled to the park with a group of other girls my age, by foot. We were members of the Brigíns, a girl guide society. We brought mini fold up chairs to sit on for the duration of the Pope's Mass. Approximately 1.25 million people gathered to see the Holy Father that day.[3] The whole event made a lasting impression on me so I felt very determined to try and ensure that my own family would be in the Phoenix Park to greet Pope Francis, an event they were also unlikely to forget.

Even before the date of his arrival, I could see God's grace at work. I had of course doubts and hesitations about if we would be able to go, managing the children, two of them older teenagers etc. Nevertheless, without overthinking things I decided to book six tickets for the final mass in Croke Park. Tickets for the Pope's visit to Knock Shrine were booked out within four hours.

We had a particularly busy summer this year with our two older children now having to be driven to summer jobs. As the date drew near for the Holy Father's visit, I discovered that I hadn't booked enough tickets. I needed seven tickets to include our student visitor who came to stay with us in August.

So I advertised my requirement on our local adoration WhatsApp group and the parish newsletter – 'one extra ticket needed.' A very kind respondent offered me tickets for the festival of families on the

Saturday evening. So now I had seven tickets for Saturday, not having a clue where we would stay overnight, and still missing one ticket for the final Mass on Sunday.

Soon afterwards, the tickets arrived by email for the final Mass. When I went to print them, I discovered that I had, in fact, eight tickets to print when I thought I only had six! So now I was fully sorted with tickets for everyone for both days.

Meanwhile, my husband got work renovating an apartment in Smithfield Gate, Dublin city centre. This turned out to be where we stayed. It was barely furnished, one double bed, a couple of sofas and plenty of dust but it was perfect!! The location was about a couple of hundred yards away from where Pope Francis would be visiting the Capuchin Day Centre on Saturday the 25th August 2018.

It was as if everything had come together to ensure that our family would be able to attend the Pope's Visit in Ireland, and not just for a day but the whole weekend.

We travelled up on the Friday evening and got the last remaining parking space on the street, (which was heavily guarded by traffic police) where we were staying. God truly is wonderful. It was just at the point where - anyone with children will know

– patience was being tested and it felt cramped in the car.

Our accommodation was very near the city centre shopping area. On Saturday the children were able to walk to Henry Street via Capel Street to do some window shopping. Later in the evening, we got ready for the walk to Croke Park to see the Festival of Families. Our teenagers were a bit dubious about what the entertainment would be like. They were pleasantly surprised. Nathan Carter sang a lovely version of the song 'Everybody hurts'. Other wonderful singers included Dolores and Seán Keane and Andrea Bocelli. There were some lovely testimonials of faith in between music acts, not the least of which was from Damien and his wife and their lovely family of 10 children. Theirs was a wonderful testimony of how faith can turn lives around from the tragedy of drug addiction. I loved what Pope Francis said about love and acceptance in our families; the sorrow he expressed about sexual abuse in the Church and how up to date he was about technology with its positive potential.

On Sunday morning, we had time to relax and see the sights before the Pope celebrated the final Mass in the Pheonix Park at 3 p.m. The weather was quite dismal. A blanket of grey cloud covered the sky.

It was windy with misting rain, so we were glad of our light plastic rain covers and umbrellas. We also had lightweight fold up stools for sitting at the event. The walk was quite long to the Pope's monument area. We arrived in section F of the area cordoned off for the Mass. It was lovely. The Pope travelled among the crowds in his Pope Mobile before the Mass.

Unexpectedly, during the Sanctus (Holy Holy), the sun came out for a couple of minutes. This was very noticeable as otherwise the sky had been completely covered in grey cloud all day long. My husband noticed it too. Praise God! That wasn't the only heavenly event which occurred. Towards the end of the Mass, some people started to leave before the final blessing. This led to a trickle of more people doing the same. My own children were getting swept up in the exodus but myself and my husband remained firm that we would wait for the final blessing. Everyone was tired at this point. But we waited, received the blessing and then started to leave. Just as we were leaving, the timing couldn't have been more perfect; we saw local stands which were filled with sandwiches and bottles of water. The volunteers giving out the refreshments just seemed to appear out of nowhere and they told us to help ourselves. It reminded me so clearly of the story of Moses and the manna from Heaven. Moses said to them, *'This is the bread which the* LORD *has given you to eat.*[16] *This is the thing which the* LORD *has commanded: 'Let every man gather it according to each one's need, one omer for each person, according to the number of persons; let every man take for those who are in his tent.'* **Exodus 16:15-16.**[1] It was as if we were being rewarded for our efforts. The Lord our shepherd truly does look after his flock! The journey out of the Phoenix Park wasn't nearly as long as the walk in.. !

26th September 2018

Jesus

'I want you to write to people about my mercy. It is an unfathomable resource for all those who have strayed from me. Make me a channel of peace in your lives. Without me, you can do nothing. I want hearts of flesh, not stone. Only love will change the world.'

30th September 2018

The call to tell my story

I cannot describe adequately how God has intervened beautifully to help me to do His work.

This morning I brought the children to Esker Monastery Mass. Fr O'Rourke had a lovely sermon about the church and how God may be trying to evangelise us in new ways as the old ways haven't been working due to scandals etc. in the Church.

I was required for reading in our local Church in Newcastle, so I attended Mass again at 10 am. I was delighted when Fr Robert introduced a speaker after Mass, who was the new leader of Youth ministry in Athenry – Keith Kelly. He was one of a group of us who had gone canvassing for the Pro-Life movement in advance of the Abortion Referendum in Ireland. Keith briefly talked about his background –a troubled youth with an alcoholic father. He was expelled and got into trouble with the Gardaí on numerous occasions. The turning point came when he was eighteen years old after a trip to Medjugorje. It affected him profoundly and he had a deep conversion.

During his speech, I felt a deep calling to tell my story. In fact, I felt on fire for all of Sunday with a great urge to do something. I spoke to Father Rob afterwards about this and he said I should come to support Keith after Mass. This didn't happen for family reasons that evening, but I was in contact with Keith on many occasions after that. I spoke again with Father Rob on the phone and he quoted **Jeremiah 20:9** *'The words are fire in my belly, a burning in my bones...'* [1] and said I should speak with the other Athenry priests individually and maybe think about talking to Keith Finnegan, Galway Bay FM and Mid-West radio. It was time for me to reflect very carefully on what to do next.

5th October 2018

Time goes very quickly, so I have to ensure Jesus' work is done. 'His will be done'. I spoke with our Parish priest yesterday afternoon about reaching out to others who are considering separation/ divorce and how it has far-reaching consequences for children. I was asking for his advice about how I could help. He suggested putting pen to paper and writing a half-hour presentation for an audience at the Pastoral Centre in Athenry. I felt very at peace with our conversation and intended to do as he has suggested. As it turned out, a couple of things happened to prevent this presentation from going ahead. May God's Will be done.

6th October 2018

I went to adoration and Esker Mass as usual this Saturday morning. During the Mass, though I hadn't planned it, I felt compelled to go to Confession and felt sure the priest would announce that he would be available after Mass. He did so and by this time I knew what I was to confess. Jesus works through our Priest in the confessional. I felt that the following words were surely for me: 'Acknowledge their pain'. I had been ruminating on what theme to use for my presentation. First, it seemed obvious to me that it was to be about separation and divorce and the far-reaching consequences on children's lives. Now I am feeling that the talk or presentation or writings, whichever format Jesus wants me to use, is to be about acknowledging pain and suffering however it has been caused and how only Jesus can heal us. He provides the 'helpers' along the way if we say 'yes' to Him and surrender ourselves to Him. It's a real message of hope for those who are suffering.

Low self-esteem, hardness of heart, misplaced guilt, depression, anxiety. These are all associated with childhood trauma. How can you love well if you have a closed heart?

Before a person experiences healing, their lives tend to be all about them and their suffering. When suffering isn't offered up to Jesus, it tends to be inflicted on others in small or big ways. I thank God every day and tell Him I love Him that my heart has been healed of my childhood trauma.

And so I began writing a recollection of my steps towards healing.

Chapter Three

The First Steps Towards Healing

Christmas 2013

At Christmas time, my brother and I went shopping for presents in Galway. We often go to bookstores as part of the shopping trip. This particular year we were in Eason's and I noticed a book called the Scent of Roses by Colm Keane.[4] It was about Padre Pio, now Saint Pio, an Italian saint who bore the stigmata of Christ. He suffered many persecutions for his faith and was even forbidden to say Mass for a time. Many people were healed by Padre Pio during his lifetime. People are still being healed through his intercession long after his death in 1968.

I remember I looked at the book and flicked through the pages and thought it would be a lovely present for him to get for me for Christmas. My brother bought it for me, albeit reluctantly, as he is at a different stage in his spiritual journey!

The book gave me enormous comfort that year I remember, as we were going through a particularly trying time financially, due to the recession, like many other people. Throughout my suffering, Jesus was able to use me to help others, one at a time. All He needed was for me to say 'yes'.

After reading 'The Scent of Roses', I felt a growing connection with Padre Pio and in March of 2014, myself and my husband travelled over to Rome for a short break with a planned trip to San Giovanni Rotondo to the Shrine of Padre Pio. The trip would turn out to be very providential as my husband was about to embark on a new and very challenging business venture in a bid to replace the building company we had which was left in serious debt after the recession.

Just as the book above had caught my attention, I remembered something that I hadn't thought about for years. It was a year preceding a time in my life when there would be great upheaval. When I was about ten or eleven, my old primary school in Manor Street showed the film 'Jesus of Nazareth' directed by Franco Zefferelli in the school hall. I was deeply affected by the film. I remember they gave out raffle tickets for the book – Jesus of Nazareth[5], and I felt a great sense of anticipation when they were calling out the raffle ticket numbers. I was sure I had won the book before they called out my name. Now

I realise it was a gift from Jesus to me. When I went home that day, I remember sitting at the kitchen table crying bitterly for Jesus, what they did to Him, the terrible suffering He went through. My father was there and comforted me.

Later, there were other things that happened coming up to the separation of my parents. There was an art competition in school in sixth class. While other children drew simple pictures you would expect of twelve or thirteen years olds, I sketched a picture of the Pieta – it's a sculpture of the dead Christ in his mother's arms sculpted by Michelangelo. The sculpture is housed in St. Peter's Basilica, Vatican City. I won a prize for my sketch.

I also remember, one day, kneeling in front of Our Lady's statue in my classroom praying. I didn't care that two other children were there giggling at me.

Jesus came into my artwork later in secondary school. I was asked to paint a picture of Jesus for a school Mass… I hadn't thought about any of this until after my healing.

March 2014

Visit to Shrine of Padre Pio

The Shrine of Padre Pio in San Giovanni Rotondo, southern Italy, is the second-most visited Catholic shrine in the world. It holds the tomb of St Padre Pio of Pietrelcina, a Capuchin friar, priest and mystic known for his devotion to God, care of the sick, and supernatural gifts including the reading of souls, prophecy, bilocation, the odour of sanctity, discernment of spirits, living on very little sleep, miraculous healings, personal visits from Jesus and Mary and daily communication with his guardian angel. Padre Pio's most famous spiritual gift is the stigmata, which he received in 1918 while praying before a crucifix. He died in 1968 and was declared a saint in 2002.[6] (padrepio.ie) In Catholic Christian terms, a mystic is someone who is committed to the search for a deeper contact with God. Padre Pio had a great devotion to Our Lady and implored people to pray regularly to her and their guardian angels.

After two days sightseeing in Rome, we travelled to Foggia by train which took two hours and fifty minutes and then from Foggia to San Giovanni Rotondo by bus for the remainder of the journey, about forty minutes.

It was not peak pilgrimage season so was lovely and quiet and it was easy to get around. The next morning we walked from the local hotel we were staying in, to the Shrine. We entered the church of Our Lady of Grace where Padre Pio is entombed. I will never forget the feeling of sorrow that hit me when we descended the ramp to the tomb of St Pio. It was as though Padre Pio was calling out to me to help me. His body is incorrupt, and is encased in a glass dome. It is the custom of visitors to pray to him there and rub religious articles such as medals and rosary beads on his tomb. It was a very profound experience. Later we went to confession to an English speaking priest and had religious articles including rosary beads, Padre Pio medals and miraculous medals blessed by the priest.

The real graces came after we returned home to Ireland though not in the way we imagined. My husband went ahead with his new business venture, setting up a new restaurant, which involved him working long hours away from home. Life went back to a hectic pace of substitute teaching for me in different schools and looking after our four young children.

It was a very difficult year with a new, unfamiliar business which had high risk attached to it. Eamon was very good at designing the layout and décor of the restaurant because of his building background, but as you know, the food business can be very fickle and attracting and keeping customers takes a lot of work and experience.

After our trip to Padre Pio's Shrine, he always kept a tiny Padre Pio medal in his wallet and I remember him being concerned when he had lost it. So it was a real surprise three to four weeks later when he spotted the medal on the ground directly outside the back door of the restaurant premises on a road which is regularly cleaned and swept (other businesses put their rubbish out there too) every day. It gave us consolation during a very stressful time.

One night we had a break-in, at the restaurant. Luckily there wasn't too much damage done. Following on from that incident we both decided to put Padre Pio medals and crucifixes on top of the back door architrave to protect it from further intruders and thankfully there were no further break-ins after that.

Around this time we also started attending mass in Galway Cathedral as a family. I used to bring the children in to 12.30 mass and meet Eamon in there. He would be coming from a late shift at the restaurant. One Sunday my youngest son was flicking through one of the books of Mass readings. (There are hundreds of them on the shelves at the end of the pews.) As he was looking through it he noticed a leaflet had fallen out of it onto the floor. He picked it up and showed it to me. At first it didn't register with me as I was focused on the Mass but when I looked again I saw it was a leaflet with a prayer to St Pio and a relic also embedded in the page. It was dated 1971. I felt that it was a gift from Padre Pio![7]

On another occasion, a man who used to work for Eamon told us that his wife's sister had breast cancer. I know his wife to chat to casually. She was working in an insurance company at the time. One day I had to visit the same insurance company to renew a policy. The woman was working there that day. She renewed the policy for me and I asked her about her sister. She said she was pretty down about it and was still undergoing treatment. I could feel the Holy Spirit at work and I felt prompted to tell her about Padre Pio and his association with many healings, both spiritual and physical. I had a Padre Pio medal with me and a prayer leaflet. I think I must have said all the right things because she seemed really hopeful and said she would definitely give the medal to her sister. I met her again a few years later at our local swimming pool and asked her how her sister was doing. She said she was doing great, that the cancer was gone and she credited the cure to a Padre Pio medal someone gave her which she wore at all times next to her breast. Praise God!

Little did I know I would shortly be embarking on my own journey to recovery!

The Road to Recovery – Autumn 2014

In my life experience, no amount of self-help books, meditation or well-meaning friends would provide the answer to healing brokenness.

As the old saying goes: 'Aithníonn ciaróg ciaróg eile', or 'it takes one to know one'. In other words what better person, who is a follower of Christ, than the person who has been broken by suffering and then has been healed by Christ, to recognise and help the broken-hearted on their journey to Christ.

It took the courage of a lovely holy woman living locally to reach out and take a chance to help me in the Autumn of 2014. She is a very prayerful lady. She knew me to see in the Church. She literally came up to me in the Church car park and said straight out that she knew I was broken and in need of healing. I had noticed her before and we may have said hello on the odd occasion, so she wasn't a complete stranger to me. That was the start of the healing process. Just like that. We met after that for coffee and on other occasions in the Church or out walking. She explained that she could see the brokenness in me because I reminded her of herself when she was my age.

This lady is very close to Jesus and Mary and has wonderful faith. She advised me to go the see a Christian Counsellor at the Redemptorist Monastery in Esker. I did hesitate about this initially, because, to be honest, I felt I wasn't very deserving of the help. I didn't know how much Jesus loved me - as He does each and every one of us - at that stage. What did appeal though, was that I would be getting 'Christian' counselling. I had only ever attended one counselling session with a layperson prior to that and came out feeling the counsellor was in greater need of healing than I was! Also, I felt that counselling which is not Christ centred is more about coping strategies and not healing.

The first few sessions with the counsellor, a Redemptorist priest, were very tough of necessity, the hurt of my past was pouring out of me, though thankfully in a very safe environment. Though I have to admit I did feel awkward at times and a little ashamed that I was in need of help at all. After all, there were other people living in much worse situations than I was, right? In between sessions which were maybe once per week or fortnight, I was going to Adoration and the Rosary Group regularly. This really sustained me. Before one particular session with the counsellor I remember sitting in front of the Blessed Sacrament in the Adoration Chapel for a short visit as I was early for my appointment. I felt a beautiful pressure on my head. It was tangible, very comforting, light, but very definite. At one point, my head was tilted slightly to one side, such was the effect of this comforting physical presence. I was literally rooted to the spot with no desire to leave.

Meanwhile, I was talking with the lady who was helping me, occasionally on the phone. I remember one particular conversation where her reassurance was invaluable. I was close to quitting the counselling as the pain of the healing (like peeling back layers of an onion) was getting to me and I was beginning to question what I had let myself in for. She said I would be feeling much better by Christmas. I hung onto those words – when you are suffering, you cling onto any words of hope. It did the trick. By Christmas, I had begun to turn a corner.

Emmanuel House, Clonfert

In between counselling sessions, I found myself accompanying two other ladies to Emmanuel House in Clonfert to Eddie Stones' Healing mission. Again, and I can't emphasise this enough, if you say 'yes' to Jesus, He will provide the 'helpers' along the way. I was very nervous the first time as I wasn't as firm in the faith as I am now. The Healing mission involves confession, Holy Mass, rosary and invoking the Holy Spirit through Divine praises and speaking in tongues. After a few sessions, I found I too was speaking in tongues.

During the last week of the Healing Mission, I felt an unspeakable sorrow. I didn't know why I felt so sad as I went up for the laying on of hands. Just as it was my turn, I burst out crying. The priest and nun who were laying hands on me brought me down to the back of the centre, spoke with me and comforted me. It was revealed to me in that moment that my sadness was due to the day I was separated forever from my brother. I was twelve years old and he was only eight years old. They were so lovely to me. The priest said he could see clearly Jesus covering a little girl protectively with his cloak. Praise God! This was another stage along the path to conversion.

The gradual nature of healing can be also be seen in a well-known gospel story where Jesus heals the blind man at Bethsaida. (**Mark 8:22-25**). When He placed his hands on the eyes of the blind man the first time, all the blind man could see were people that looked like trees walking about. Jesus had to place his hands on the man's eyes a second time in order for him to see clearly. And so it is with other types of healing. The next significant event on my own healing journey was the pilgrimage to Medjugorje.

Easter 2015 - Medjugorje

A pilgrimage is an invaluable way to restore and renew your faith. If we don't push ourselves out of our comfort zone, how will we ever grow in our faith and learn new truths about Jesus? Let me tell you how I eventually got to go to Medjugorje. I was attending a rosary group on a regular basis while working part-time in 2014 and 2015. I had been thinking of going to Medjugorje on a number of occasions for about a year when I saw a notice for a meeting about an upcoming trip with Jim Browne and Fr Benny in the Parish newsletter.

It was set for Easter 2015. I had a strong urge to go, but lots of negative thoughts entered my head about why I shouldn't go, you know that nagging voice speaking of every excuse not to do something. I met another lady at the meeting who I knew from hurling circles. Jim's talk was very inspiring. He had been through a physically abusive childhood and was a successful businessman but drawn to excess and deeply in need of healing. He found this in Medjugorje and felt a calling to tell others about his experience in order to help them.

At the end of the meeting, people stayed behind to speak further with Jim. I battled within myself whether to stay or go. I decided to leave the meeting. I excused myself and went to the bathroom. Then I noticed I had no handbag. I had left it in the meeting room. So I had to go back in to retrieve it. I felt embarrassed at the thought of leaving again, but also I thought it was a sign, when I left my handbag behind that I was meant to stay. This time I stayed to talk with Jim with the others. The last thing I said, and it was within earshot of Fr Benny, was: 'I must go some time.' Fr Benny replied 'Better sooner than later'. For some reason, this simple statement stuck with me and wouldn't leave my mind after that. Within a short space of time, I was booked onto that Easter trip with the other lady I knew. The time was right for her also. Praise God!

One thing I have found and I know others will concur on this, if a pilgrimage is meant to be, that is, if it is God's work the obstacles real or imagined will fall away one by one. That was the way with Medjugorje and a few years later, the Holy Land. I had no trouble getting the money together, getting the children minded, etc. and I was a substitute teacher, so I wasn't working during the Easter holidays.

Our pilgrimage set off from Athenry to Dublin airport and from there we flew to Dubrovnik. A bus took us for the remainder of the journey to Medjugorje. Fr Benny led the rosary as the bus approached Medjugorje. There were two of us sharing the room in half-board accommodation 5-minute walk from St James's church. I remember that we were up early in the morning every day of the week for breakfast, prayers and visits to different places.

One trip that really stands out in my mind was the visit to the visionary Vicka's house.[8] She prayed from the balcony of her home and led us in quiet prayer. It was very peaceful. She has a beautiful, joyful smile. After the prayers, I had a chance to shake her hand a number of times. It was very emotional.

Another place which had a great impact on everyone was the Cenacolo centre for reformed drug addicts set up by Mother Elvira. We also visited another church in a little village called Šurmanci, hidden away in the mountains. There is a miraculous icon of Jesus and Mary here. I remember poor children were selling polished stones with holy pictures painted on them and handmade rosary beads. They were so cheap to us, but that money meant a lot to them and their families.

We witnessed the miracle of the weeping statue of the Resurrected Christ.[9] This is a miracle that everyone who visits Medjugorje can see for themselves. The day we went down there after the Stations of the Cross, water (tears) were oozing from the side of the right knee and the back of the left thigh. Scientists are unable to explain the phenomenon. The day we were there was cloudless and the ground and atmosphere were very dry. People were queuing up with little white napkins to soak them with the tears of Christ. These little napkins are kept by people for their families and to give as gifts to others for healing purposes.

14th October 2018

As I write I am thinking of others and how their conversion to Christ might look like on the outside. From the loud, opinionated person who becomes quiet and humble and listens more, to the quiet nervous soul who becomes more confident to speak up in company, no longer afraid of the opinions of others....

Yesterday before work, I met a woman whose child I used to teach. Actually, I first met her years ago when our eldest children were babies in the mother and toddler group in Athenry. We both arrived in the school car park at the same time.

This lady spoke to me of how her family had stopped going to Mass. Prior to her telling me this I had been talking to her about how the church was looking for more Adorers for the adoration of the Blessed sacrament and the great work of the Esker Redemptorists. She explained that her husband doesn't go to Mass and doesn't believe. She says he's quite angry about it. I told her that after I came back from the Holy Land, my husband was converted and started going to Adoration every week as well as going to Mass. She knows now that it will be her - with God's help - who brings her family, especially her husband through this crisis of faith, through her prayers, suffering and example. We spoke about Medjugorje. She says she has been thinking of going for a while and I told her the above story of the meeting I went to about Medjugorje. I prayed that she would get a chance to go.

17th October 2018

Recalling Medjugorje continued…

This morning I woke early at 5 am and waited to drift off to sleep. Almost every morning on waking,

I thank Jesus and God and tell them that I love them and thank them for everything. Increasingly I offer up all my sufferings for the day and the days ahead for the salvation of souls. This morning I woke up to the hymn of 'Soul of my Saviour, sanctify my breast..' I felt great love in my heart for Jesus when I heard these words. I asked Jesus did he want me to get up and write and He said He did.

So to take up again my Easter 2015 pilgrimage to Medjugorje, One morning I was helping my friend in our apartment to draft a letter of reply to a job she had been offered in Ireland. It would mean a lot to her and her family as she had been out of work for over a year. In Medjugorje, Our Lady appears to Vicka, one of the six visionaries every day at 6.40 pm Irish time. This particular evening I did not want to miss the Holy Mass in St James' church, at the time when the apparition would be taking place, though not in the Church itself but rather wherever Vicka was that evening.

The apartment where we were staying was about seven minutes' walk away from the Church and time was pushing on. The Mass would commence at 6.30 pm, but my friend needed a second opinion on an email she was drafting to a future employer. I had worked in Personnel and therefore knew something about details of employment contracts, etc. I didn't want to leave her while she was composing the email which would help her with her future career. But I felt a great sense of urgency to get down to the Church. We had just finished working on an email when I quickly made my way down to St James' church. In fact, I was running.

I felt a great sense of anticipation as I had done when I was a child having the winning raffle ticket for the book Jesus of Nazareth. I knew something was going to happen - that I would see something. (I had been praying that I would witness a miracle at some point during the pilgrimage.) It was after 6.40 p.m. at this point, so I remember distinctly apologising to Our Lady for being late as I ran up the steps of the Church and hurried indoors. The Church was packed. I stood among other people standing at the back of the Church. I had my phone switched on and ready to record whatever was going to happen. My heart was thumping with anticipation. I pressed record. The Holy Holy was being sung and during it, I could see light behind the tabernacle getting gradually larger and larger in a circular shape. The light radiated from the edges of the circle. At the 19 seconds part of my recording as the Holy Holy was being sung, a supernatural light flooded the Church which seemed to emanate from the circular light behind the tabernacle. The singing continued and at the 1 minute and 19 seconds point in the recording, exactly one minute later, a brilliant pulsating light, like a heart beat, came from the circular light filling the whole Church, illuminating it in a very bright golden white light for a few seconds. The light though brilliant, was not blinding. I was very overcome throughout all of this, but I kept my phone up high and kept recording. I looked around me to see who else could see this wonderful vision and nobody seemed to notice except one young man a few rows ahead of me. He was looking around also. The singing of the Holy Holy ended and I stopped recording at the two minutes point. The Holy Mass continued on as normal after that.

It would be two years later before I finally plucked up the courage to put my video recording on YouTube.[10] Before this I was so concerned with what other people would think of me – would they think I was mad, what makes you so special etc.. A few people were very keen to see the video on the Pilgrimage. I was very careful not to push it on anyone. The person who stands out most in her reaction was one of the Medjugorje Pilgrimage Guides who is in St James' Church nearly every day. She said she never saw anything like it there before. Her eyes opened wide when she looked at it. My family and extended family saw a huge change in me when I returned from Medjugorje. Some were very receptive and others more sceptical. So it was an emotional roller coaster.

Time to go now and get ready for a new day.

'*Thank you, God, Jesus, Mary and Saint Joseph and all the angels and saints in Heaven for getting me out of bed this morning. Please keep me alert and obedient to your call.*'

22nd October 2018

Unusually it is after school as I write today. I have a few minutes' peace in the sitting room as the kids are out playing and it's a lovely still autumn evening. It was a very hectic weekend with children's activities and sports. We had a visitor to my school during the week selling Irish books and when she was finished her pitch she casually spoke about her grand aunt Mary Byrne being one of the visionaries in Knock. I asked her to tell the story of Knock as she had heard it passed down through the generations. It was lovely to have a 'living' witness connected to the story in some way and the children were very interested. Meanwhile our local priest called in to meet the children who are making their Confirmation and so the story about Knock continued between our visitors over a cup of tea!

28th October 2018

The Fourth Commandment

I am suffering a lot with general physical discomfort over the past few days. When this happens, it's hard to feel close to the Lord and to pray consistently and not to get bogged down with worldly matters. Notwithstanding, I know from previous experience that it is when you are suffering that Our Lord can achieve his best work. I wait patiently for Jesus and Mary to guide me this morning. It is early and the family are still asleep. I have my bible beside me, my Catholic Catechism (the newly revised 2014 version) beautifully written with and introduction to each chapter describing a saint or blessed person from different centuries in very simple and clear language. Each chapter has questions at the end to help you assimilate the information.

Coming from a broken home I have sometimes struggled with the fourth commandment – 'honour your father and your mother.' In the Penny Catechism it states to honour parents in all that is not sin.[11] I remember feeling very reassured when I read this the first time. If children have parents who are suffering from emotional wounds themselves due to their own or another's sin they may not be able to engage fully with their children in a Christian way. Before I started on my own healing journey, I would have carried a lot of guilt about not being able 'to fix' my parents problems. Now I realise that their journey to God is different from mine and that the best thing I can do for them is keep them always in my prayers.

Sometimes a period of absence will work best between parents and their adult children while they are on that journey. I pray that Jesus and Mary will continue to guide me and inspire me to keep in contact with them at the right times and in appropriate ways.

'*In our permissive culture, love is sometimes so romanticised that it is separated from sacrifice. Because of this, tough moral choices cannot be faced. The absence of sacrificial love dooms the possibility of an authentic moral life.*' (**Page 352 Irish Catholic Catechism for adults**).[12]

When sacrificial love is abandoned, for example in the dissolution of the marriage - the door is opened to a whole host of other sins like adultery, avoidance of duty, lack of care for the children, avoidance of extended family members etc. In addition, there are the far-reaching consequences of a marriage break up for the couple themselves and for their children: lack of solid moral foundation shown by example in marriage and parental responsibility; confusion about right and wrong in family and relationship matters; turbulent emotions when talking about families, etc.

Just as I finish this morning, I look at a quote from St Faustina's diary no. 489. She was praying the Rosary when she was thinking about a meeting with Fr Andrasz the following day when fear seized her at the sight of her 'misery and incapability, and of the greatness of God's work.' Then Jesus said to her *'Why are you afraid to do My Will? Will I not help you as I have done thus far?'* [13] This is very reassuring if we are ever in doubt about doing God's Will. Please God help me to do your Will in total obedience. I see Padre Pio calling me to finish now and tend to the family.

'Thank you Jesus and Mary and all the angels and saints in heaven.'

7th November 2018

'Dear Jesus,

Thank you for the lovely week I had with my family. Thank you that I was able to help my friend with your guidance. Thank you for the special love I have with my husband and help me to continue to love him as you want me to dear Jesus. Especially help me to love all my family and friends and co-workers unconditionally with Your heart and to see You in my neighbour.'

It feels as if it has been a long time since I wrote last for Jesus. I feel the Lord's peace. Not long ago, when at a match my son was playing in, I bumped into a neighbour of mine who has children of similar ages to mine. It turned out that her brother was very sick with cancer and was not likely to get better. She was crying because she wanted him to have some peace before he died, and he wasn't at peace. I asked her would she like some blessed religious articles for him. She asked me to pray for him and light a candle for him. A couple of days later I gave my daughter blessed rosary beads from the Holy Land and a green scapular which is known to aid conversion and healing from illness when the prayer is recited, to give to the neighbour's daughter in school. About a week later, I was in Galway Cathedral buying an updated version of the adult Catholic Catechism. As I was leaving the Cathedral, I remembered to light a candle for my neighbour's brother. I walked down the corridor. On my left, on the way out were the confessional booths. Straight in front of me was the candle stand. I was just lighting the candle when I heard a 'ping' go off in my bag. It was my phone with a text message from the neighbour thanking me for the rosary beads and scapular… As soon as I left the

Church, I texted her back to explain this wonderful coincidence. Thank you Jesus, for your perfect timing in matters of faith. A week or so later, I met her unexpectedly and I repeated to her what had happened. I added that I had been in the Cathedral book shop a few minutes before lighting the candle buying a newly updated Catholic Catechism which was beautifully written in modern language which would appeal to people in these times (maybe a seed was sown there too, God knows!) She confirmed that her brother had had a good week and was more at peace in himself. Praise God!

'Thank you God for everything!'

18th November 2018

'Thank you Jesus and Our Lady that you have called me to write again. Our Parish Priest, Fr Brendan, had a stroke a couple of weeks ago and is now recovering in hospital. Please God may he make a full recovery and may his sufferings be used for the salvation of souls according to Your Will.

I am at a crossroads dear Jesus about the next step to take in relation to doing Your Will while I am on earth.'

At times I feel a sense of urgency to take a particular direction only to be held back due to family or work commitments. I know that I can also offer these very valuable efforts to God and maybe that's all He requires of me right now, but I remain attentive to the promptings of the Holy Spirit. I can't help but hear the pleas of Our Lady in the messages she reveals to the visionaries and mystics. What if we all sit back and expect someone else to promote God's healing and mercy to other sinners? We are here to save souls, are we not, through our prayers, corporal and spiritual works? Each of us has a gift to use for God in a particular area *'if it is to serve, we should serve; if it is to teach we should teach..'* **Romans 12:7** [1] We know the areas we are gifted in by personal experience. We need to act on the inner promptings of the Lord.

Last week I attended a training course during which I had a strong inner prompting from the Lord which I get sometimes. I now recognise these promptings as being for my own good or someone else's and should not be ignored. I was urged to ring two people to discuss a work-related issue. I was made aware that if I rang, I would get through straight away which I did. Jesus and Mary help us with so many things, even small things, if we are conscious of their presence and accept their guidance. They also allow trials sometimes to help us to grow in our faith.

A vibrant faith is one which is constantly developing and being tried, (not beyond our capabilities though). Jesus will never test us beyond our limitations. I can see parallels in the classroom. As teachers, we are always striving to achieve the best in our pupils – we have to try different methods to help them learn. At times we have to discipline them to get them to be more attentive and settle down to their work. This is not a bad thing as it shows we care for them. Similarly, God cares even more so for us and He will do what it takes to guide us home. So, think of some trials you have had in your life. Did you learn from them? On reflection, was God trying to reach you in some way?

I also remember one evening I was dozing on the sofa a number of years ago. I remember clearly it was a Sunday evening. I woke up from my slumber with an abrupt start. I felt an urgent prompting to ring my Dad. I wouldn't normally have rung at this particular time. When I rang, I asked Dad straight away was there something wrong. He was in a bad way as he had just been given the news that a very close friend of his was very sick with a brain tumour and was given a short time to live. He was very grateful to have someone to talk to about it. Other times I have felt an urgent prompting to pray for someone who might be in trouble. I remember praying for a teacher who told me she had visited a 'white witch'. I just woke one night sometime after that and prayed for her. It's obedience in the small things that count. One small act of kindness, a prayer, lighting a candle, acting on an interior prompt. If we align our lives with God who is love itself, who can refuse Him? *'If God be for us, who can be against us?'* **Romans 8:31**[1]

8th December 2018

The Feast of the Immaculate Conception of Mary

'Christ has no body now but yours. No hands, no feet on earth but yours. Yours are the eyes through which he looks compassion on this world. Yours are the feet with which he walks to do good. Yours are the hands through which he blesses all the world. Yours are the hands, yours are the feet, yours are the eyes, you are his body. Christ has no body now on earth but yours.' **St Teresa of Avila.**[14] This quote reminds me that we all have a chance to be modern-day apostles of Christ using our God-given gifts. Let's reach out in faith and be not afraid.

It is a number of weeks ago since I felt inspired to write. I have accepted that the timing wasn't right. I accept God's Will in all situations. A few days ago I bumped into a fellow adorer during Adoration whom I met at a Christian seminar in Galway last year. I had been thinking of this person as I had borrowed books from him and needed to return them. I had a faith-related question that had been annoying me for the past number of weeks. He found a passage in a holy book for me which gave me peace and clarity about my query. The Lord often uses holy people to help us on our journey. Always be alert to the prompting of the Holy Spirit. You will usually feel at peace with yourself when the Spirit is at work unless of course, the Holy Spirit wants you to act, in which case, you will feel a more urgent prompting to act than usual! When this happens, you may be required to act out of your comfort zone. It may be a phone call you have to make, or you see someone in need and Jesus wants you to reach out in some way to that person, it could be a warning that you are treading on dangerous territory or you are becoming complacent in some area of your life. My experience is that when the Lord wants you to do something, He will give you the grace of perseverance to carry out His Will. You only have to say 'Yes'. *'He will never leave you nor forsake you. Do not be afraid; do not be discouraged...'***Deuteronomy 31:8**[1]

Prayer

'Thank you Mary, a Mhuire Mháthair O Immaculate Conception for loving us and guiding us to Jesus.'

19ᵗʰ December 2018

I have but a short time to write this morning. I felt a call during the previous night to get up and write for Jesus but am sorry to say I ignored the call in favour of a warm bed. How weak are we mortal human beings……? The Spirit is willing but the flesh is weak!

We are really looking forward to Christmas. It is windy and quite mild weather. All are asleep as I wait here to write for Jesus.

Forgiveness

Here are a few inspirations about forgiveness. The forgettable and forgivable transgressions are for example where someone has hurt us with a short outburst of temper due to some frustration or from general suffering in life, which is followed up by an apology or an action showing remorse.

These transgressions do not store in our hearts quite so much as very personal and sustained attacks on our character especially from a loved one e.g. a parent/child relationship or other close relationship.

Forgiveness is an ongoing process but it is a necessary act of the will and not just based on how we feel. Sometimes we think we have forgiven a certain person totally for past hurts. This could be where a person's jealous or envious nature is the cause of their hurting us.

The truth is even if we have forgiven the person(s) who hurt us the most, we will still have to be aware that that person may not be healed yet for God's own reasons and we may or may not be part of their healing. The wonderful thing I have found on my own faith journey is that Jesus will bring the right people and situations into our lives to help us along the way. You will know when you have a sense of joy and peace. Sometimes He will allow another person to cross your path who is similar to the relative who caused you great pain in your life for you to help with their journey to healing and faith. It is like if He can't use you in one area, you want to fix, e.g. a family situation, He will provide you with another one which has some similarities but is not a challenge you won't be able to overcome. Remember He will never test you beyond your limits! Also remember to 'let' Jesus work through you. Our will must not interfere with God's Will. Simply think about the Lord's prayer: Our Father, Who art in Heaven, Hallowed be Thy name, Thy Kingdom come, Thy Will be done, On earth as it is in Heaven, Give us this day Our daily bread and **forgive <u>us</u> our trespasses as we forgive <u>those</u> who trespass against us** and lead us not into temptation (or bring us not to hard testing) but deliver us from evil. Amen.

An endnote about forgiveness: while the person who has hurt you is still in your life pray to Jesus to protect you, against situations from happening in communications with that person, which will leave you feeling vulnerable or hurt. This may involve time apart from this person and not engaging in hurtful communications with them while wishing them well and God's peace to them from your heart. God will give you the strength to do this. Keep your heart open.

Further end note, see **us** and **those** in the Lord's Prayer. We've often heard of the phrase 'us' and 'them'. The Lord is well aware of our fallen nature and that 'we' are as in need of forgiveness as 'the ones' whom we need to forgive! So let that always be our awareness too that 'we' have hurt others….

Chapter Four

Ongoing Conversion

The conversion experience allows us to see not only the faults of others, but even more importantly our own faults seen through our own eyes and not told to us by others. I remember one night not long after I came back from Medjugorje I cried when I realised all my own sins and the ways in which I had hurt people. It was as if they became as clear as day to me. The great thing though about this is we can do something about it when we know what our sins are. Confession becomes a very important part of your life. It prevents a hardening of the heart. Layers of sin build up the longer you leave facing confession. It's not called one of the sacraments without reason!

'I thirst'

Yesterday I was feeling particularly lonely for a close relative. One could almost say I had a deep longing for this person. Last night I was doing day 17 of my consecration to Mary, 33 days of Morning Glory written by Fr Michael Gaitley.[15] When I read the piece by Mother Teresa, I felt I understood 'a tiny bit' of what Jesus feels when he 'thirsts' for souls, albeit in my limited human way.

Mother Teresa wrote: *'Our Lady was the first person to hear Jesus' cry "I Thirst" with St John and I am sure Mary Magdalen. Because Our Lady was there on Calvary, she knows how real, how deep His longing for you and for the poor is. Do we know? Do we feel as she? Ask her to teach….Her role is to bring you face to face, as John and Magdalen, with love in the heart of Jesus crucified. Before it was Our Lady pleading with Mother, now it is Mother in her name pleading with you—"listen to Jesus thirst."'*

Jesus wants us to save souls because he 'thirsts' for souls! In what ways can we help Jesus save souls? Especially in times when people are turning away from the Church? The people who have experienced conversion are 'called' to help or spread the good news that Jesus is fully present in our lives today if we will just open our hearts to Him. Jesus is sending 'us' out to spread the news of His kingdom using **our** particular gifts.

'Thank you Jesus.'

St Stephen's Day - 26th December 2018

Our gifts

I love this verse of the letter from St Paul to the Romans 12:2. *'Do not conform yourselves to the standards of this world, but let God transform you inwardly by a complete change of your mind. Then you will be able to know the will of God – what is good and is pleasing to him and is perfect.'*

St Paul goes on to say: *'.We are to use our different gifts in accordance with the grace God has given us. If our gift is to speak God's message, we should do it according to the faith we have; if it is to serve, we should serve, if it is to teach, we should teach, if it is to encourage others, we should do so. Whoever shares with others should do it generously, whoever has authority should work hard; whoever shows kindness to others should do it cheerfully.'* **Romans 12:6 – 8**[1]

27th December 2018

The Narrow Gate

Matthew 7:13-14. *'Enter through the narrow gate. For wide is the gate and broad is the road that leads to destruction, and many enter through it. But small is the gate and narrow is the road that leads to life, and only a few find it.'* [1]

Today I discovered an article from the SMA (Society for the African Missions) international website.[16] It was an obituary of Father John Michael Monahan, my uncle, who died before I was born.

He was a missionary priest who was assigned to the diocese of Ibadan in Southwest Nigeria for the SMA Ireland. I had, in fact, tried to look up information about him previously as I had heard many years before that he had been assigned to the Missions in Africa and had been involved in a serious car accident there. It was only when I found out the name of the order he was with that I came across his obituary.

On October 1958, four months after his ordination, Father John set sail for Ibadan. John came to Nigeria at a time of great development in the church when the seed sown in the early decades of the century was being reaped. He spent a year undergoing induction training in the Tyrocinium at St Leo's, Ibadan which involved learning local languages, learning local culture and undertaking supervised pastoral activity. In 1959 he received his first substantive appointment teaching philosophy in St Peter and Paul's regional seminary.

On the 2nd November 1962, scarcely four years later, he died in a motor accident on the road back from Lagos to Ibadan with another priest who survived. He was travelling on the passenger side of the car. The car they were travelling in collided with an unlit parked lorry. Fr John later died of his injuries in Shagamu hospital. May he rest in peace. He was buried in the grounds of St Theresa's minor seminary at Oke Are, near the site of the earliest mission in Ibadan founded in 1895.

My mother was staying with us for Christmas so I printed off the article and gave her a copy of it. She was obviously quite emotional about the story as she remembers him as being a lovely calm 'peace making' older brother in a house with nine children! She says, they would be fighting a lot and he would be trying to study in an adjoining room. He would never lose his temper with them and would cajole them into good behaviour! Sadly his mother, my maternal grandmother, passed away only three weeks before he died, from a brain haemorrhage. My mother remembers her calling out for John in her delirious state towards the end of her life, repeatedly saying 'poor Johnny, poor Johnny!' It was as if she knew something was going to happen to him...

Isaiah 57:1-2. *'The righteous perish, and no one takes it to heart; the devout are taken away, and no one understands that the righteous are taken to be spared from evil. Those who walk uprightly enter into peace; they find rest as they lie in death.'* [1]

28th December 2018

'Dear Jesus, I am waiting here to write for you. Thank you for the lovely Christmas which was especially peaceful this year.'

Despite my sufferings today, I feel Jesus is calling me to write. I couldn't settle until I started my work for Jesus. I sometimes get plagued with doubts about my abilities, but I remind myself that God is love and His love produces fruits of the Holy Spirit which are love, joy, peace, patience, goodness, gentleness, faithfulness, kindness and self-control. So my doubts are not part of His Divine Plan for me. In Jesus name 'I rebuke Satan and all the wicked spirits who roam the world seeking the ruin of souls.'(part of prayer to St Michael the Archangel.)[17] My advance prayer is to ask Jesus to offer up my sufferings for souls who are in need of saving grace. I say 'advance' because when you are in the throes of suffering it is easy to forget to pray or offer up sufferings and thank God for them etc.

Sometimes I write with great consolations from Jesus and the Blessed Mother. Other times the experience is barren and the words seem heavy. I accept this Lord and I soldier on for you.

I had a wonderful consolation from a telephone conversation with my Dad yesterday though. I was enquiring about my Granny Pauline who passed away when I was small. I had heard that she was quite religious. In fact, he told me that she wore the brown scapular for most of her life.

My heart skipped a beat when I heard this. I had just had my own family enrolled in the brown scapular of Mount Carmel last summer in Loughrea Carmelite Abbey. No person suggested I do this, but I had a strong conviction to do so after reading St Therese's book 'The Little Way' during the summer.

I suspect enrolling families in the brown scapular is not done so much these days. In addition to wearing the scapular, there are three requirements to gain the Sabbatine Privilege of salvation. They are 'prayer, penance and chastity according to one's state in life. All three are ingredients of a sincere Christian life, and hence of authentic devotion to Our Lady.' (www.ocarm.org)[18] God bless Granny Pauline! Granny was buried in the brown habit of the Third Order of Carmelites.

A Brief History of the Carmelite Order

In an apparition of the Virgin Mary to St Simon Stock in the mid-thirteenth century, Our Lady said: *'This will be for you and for all Carmelites the privilege, that he who dies in this habit will be saved'…. 'The faithful Carmelite religious is bound by his vows and constitutions to live a life of renunciation, dedication to prayer, and love of God and neighbour'....'* Eventually, the Carmelite Order, which consisted of a First Order (priests and friars) a Second Order, (nuns), expanded to include a Third Order of Laity, who commit themselves to *'prayer and good works, a commitment signified by the devotional brown scapular.'* (P 42, 33 days to Morning Glory).[19]

It is worthy of note that Our Lady appeared in the Carmelite habit to the children of Fatima wearing the Brown scapular in her final apparition to them on 13th October 1917 (p. 33 The message of Fatima – Lucia speaks.)[20]

Note – When you decide to accept God's call, He will show you the way - His Will for your life. He will show you signs that you will notice because you are alert to His help. It will not be like before when you didn't trust Him or never asked Him for help.

29th December 2018

Jesus

'Write about my mercy for sinners.'

Lack of understanding of God's mercy holds sinners back from reconciling with the one true God. He is everyone's God. Just as a parent forgives their child for bad behaviour so too God forgives us for our trespasses because of His unconditional love for us.

Prayer

'Thank you Jesus, for your great love and mercy. We are unworthy sinners; please help us to stay committed to Your Will for our lives. Come Holy Spirit, help us to live like Jesus and not sin again.'

Trip to the Holy Land June/July 2017

I am finally getting to write about the trip to the Holy Land. I had often seen Fr Benny's trips to the Holy Land advertised every year in the Parish newsletter. Funnily enough, it was a trip I had always imagined my husband would make someday, not myself. I also figured that my main pilgrimage was the one to Medjugorje, so maybe the Holy Land would be the trip for him. Anyway, the Lord has His own plans. I had certainly heard Fr Benny talking about the Holy Land before, but I didn't really think I would be going.

Nevertheless, a couple of months before the July 2017 trip, I felt called to go on this trip. It is an expensive trip as there is a lot of travelling and four flights involved, plus accommodation for twelve nights, a guide and bus travel and passes to all the main sites of significance in the Life of Jesus. So cost alone was a possible obstacle as I was a substitute teacher at the time and our financial situation at the time was a little precarious. There was also the problem of getting the children minded for the twelve days. However, when God wants you to do something, He will sort out the obstacles. One by one they fell away. The first obstacle to be overcome was the one about getting the children minded. My husband had just finished up work at the end of May and would be free to take care of them. The next obstacle was actually to do with safety – I looked up information about this and decided the trip would be safe enough for an organised pilgrimage. Another hesitation I had was that I was questioning my motivations, was I really supposed to go or did I imagine things? A phone call to my Dad sorted that one out. He said straightaway I should go as he had meant to go years before and never got around to it!

So I got the encouragement I needed. I also had some worries about not knowing who I was going to travel with and share accommodation with. This turned out to be fine too. I shared a room with a lovely lady from Mayo. Covering the cost was really the final one. This came in the form of an email out of the blue, from the father of a student from Spain I hosted five years earlier. (He stayed with me for

5 months to learn English when he was fifteen.) In the email, his father asked me if I would be willing to take his son for three weeks during the summer, full board. I agreed to take him and this payment covered the remaining cost of my trip. Amazingly the dates he wanted me to take his son were literally three days after my return from the Holy Land. I remember saying to my husband after reading the email that I really was meant to go on the trip. So everything worked out perfectly! Praise God!

30th December 2018

So as planned, I joined thirty three other travellers and set off on our Trip to the Holy Land on Monday 26th June departing from Dublin Airport at 16.30 stopping over in Istanbul at 22.55 for three hours and setting out again at 1.40 for our final destination, Ben Gurion Airport, Tel Aviv at 3.55. We travelled on a guided bus and arrived at the Restal Hotel in Tiberias at 7 am on the 27th June 2017. Curiously Tiberius is situated 682ft below sea level which immediately stirred my imagination - what if there was volcanic eruption or earthquake at sea nearby how would things turn out?! From the start, we were given a detailed historical account and geographical description of every area we passed through on our pilgrimage by our Guide Mutassin. Fr Benny was also very informative and regularly made us laugh with his jokes. Fr Brendan was a newcomer to the trip. He delivered some lovely sermons as did Fr Benny at the daily Masses which were celebrated on the pilgrimage.

Recalling visit to the Grotto of Gethsemane, Monday 3rd July 2017

On the 3rd of July, we had a holy hour between 8 and 9 o'clock at the Grotto of Gethsemane which has been venerated since the Byzantine Period as the place where Jesus prayed with his disciples. This was one of three places which spiritually had a great impact on me. Arriving in the garden we saw how it is now protected and fenced off. On the rock where Jesus prayed a huge sorrow filled my heart as a close family member, still living, came to mind. It was unexpected. I remember feeling the same way in San Giovanni Rotondo as we descended the ramp to the open crypt where St Padre Pio's remains were.

Recalling visit to the Benedictine Dormition Abbey, Tuesday 4th July 2017

I felt a special spiritual connection with Our Lady in the Dormition Abbey. There is a statue of Mary in repose here and this marks the place where Catholics celebrate Mary's falling asleep. I offered up prayers for two fellow pilgrims in the group after a prompting from the Holy Spirit and felt a great sense of clarity and peace here.

Recalling visit to the Church of the Holy Sepulchre, Wednesday 5th July 2017

We had Mass at 7.30 am in the Church of the Holy Sepulchre. This for me, was the highlight of the trip. It is a very beautiful and special place. It was very spiritual and I felt great clarity, all external noise seemed to be shut out. I was really able to offer up intentions to Jesus here at the foot of the Cross on the site where he was crucified. We were able to touch the ground underneath the sculpted Crucifix. I rubbed two sets of rosary beads on this area. There is a sculpture of Our Lady beside the Crucifix. Her expression is agonised. Behind Fr Kilcoyne, who was celebrating Holy Mass, is a Mosaic of Jesus being crucified. We then went downstairs to the site where Jesus was lain out afterwards. We kissed the stone He lay on. After that, we were very blessed to be able to enter Jesus's burial tomb where the resurrection took place. It is small and there is a beautiful painting of the Resurrection there. Scientists Christian and non-Christian alike believe that Jesus was buried here. There is evidence of only one man having been buried in the Holy Tomb.

Afterwards, we spoke with Fr Fergus Clarke in the inner sanctum of the Holy Sepulchre Church. He is a Franciscan priest who gave us a brief history of the Franciscans in the Holy Land and also the 'delicate' situation within the Holy Sepulchre Church with six different religious groups, Catholics, Greek Orthodox, Armenians, Syrians, Copts and Ethiopians. Fr Fergus informed us that crusaders fought to protect the crucifix site and burial site of Jesus. Later the site was covered up by Pagans with statues of Jupiter and Venus on top. This made it easier for subsequent generations to find the site of Jesus' tomb by excavating it and finding the original tomb within! Father also said that the Franciscans in the Holy Sepulchre Church get up at night to pray for the purpose of keeping the Catholic area (there are 5 other religious groups as named above) of the Church open to groups like ours to see where Jesus was crucified and buried and also to enable priests to celebrate Mass here.

4th January 2019

The train journey to Dublin - the Miraculous Medal

I've missed writing for a few days now. It was my birthday on 31st December and we had my husband's parents over for dinner on New Year's Day. It was lovely and I realise these are very special days while the grandparents are healthy and well. I travelled to Dublin on the 2nd of January to visit my Dad and my brother while my brother is still in Ireland for the Christmas period. It is difficult enough for me to pull away from home to go to Dublin because I find it a very sad and godless place, especially around Heuston station and parts of the Quays. The scourge of drugs and homelessness is very evident. It is a big contrast to the atmosphere on the train full of expectant travellers perhaps travelling to have a day out shopping or going to see a panto or the theatre or visit relatives like me.

I brought with me an article I found in the thirty three days to Morning Glory (Consecration to Mary) booklet written by Fr Michael Gaitley about the wearing of blessed sacramentals. As I mentioned earlier, my dad described how his mother had worn the brown scapular most of her life. I found this very inspiring and sensed a wonderful connection with my paternal grandmother.

I travelled on the 9.48 am train to Dublin. It was great to have a chance to pray quietly and read. Ever since my pilgrimage to Medjugorje in 2015 I have promised God that I will be a lay apostle of Jesus and try to spread the Good News in some small way by example or when I am out and about or travelling. Opportunities abounded on this particular train journey.

I came across a wonderfully documented history of the miraculous medal as revealed to St Catherine Labouré by Our Lady in 1830. The little prayer which is struck around the edges of the miraculous medal is as follows: *'O Mary, conceived without sin, pray for us who have recourse to thee.'*

The medal features Our Lady standing on a globe with her hands outstretched, fingers adorned with precious jewels with light coming from them. On the reverse side is the letter 'M' surmounted by a cross, at the foot of the cross, a bar and below all the Heart of Jesus crowned with thorns, and the Heart of Mary pierced with a sword.

Our Lady said to Catherine 'Have a medal struck after this model. Persons who wear it will have great graces, especially if they wear it around the neck.' (www.catholicism.org).[21]

When I first got on the train in Athenry, I sat at a table diagonally across from a lovely dark-haired young woman aged about twenty years old. She had a lovely smile and seemed not to mind my request to sit at the table. She said she was holding two seats for her family, one of whom was her brother and they would be getting on in Ballinasloe. I began to look up information on my phone and waited for the train to pull out. About 10 minutes into the journey the food trolley was doing the rounds. When it reached my table, I asked for a sandwich and coffee which cost just under €8. I had €7 in my purse and a €50 note. As we were in the first carriage, he didn't have any change of €50, so my train companion kindly gave me a euro to complete the purchase. I thanked her profusely and offered her a sandwich, bun etc. as a thank you but she declined.

Time passed as we listened to our phones, read, etc. The train stopped at Ballinasloe and her relatives were nowhere to be seen. She was a little anxious and rang them. It turned out they were getting on in Athlone. When they got on the train in Athlone, the woman's brother told her he had pre-booked seats for the three of them, so she moved further down the carriage. The three seats at my table didn't remain vacant for long. A woman in her early forties sat beside me with her two children, a girl and a boy aged about nine and six years. We exchanged a few words and I noticed how she was really nice to her children and how she probably liked following the latest styles from her appearance. I ascertained from a phone call she made that she was bringing them to a panto performance in Dublin. The train trundled on. It pulled into Heuston it seemed about ten minutes early, but in fact, by the time it came to a halt, it was exactly on time, 11.52 am.

At this stage, I had been happily watching a documentary on my phone about the history of the miraculous medal as detailed above. I prayed that I would do the right thing by giving the two children a blessed miraculous medal each from my handbag. I was a bit nervous, but an opportunity presented itself and I didn't want to let the moment pass. It turned out to be the right decision. Firstly the children were delighted and secondly their mother was thrilled and immediately took the medal off the younger child, 'just in case he loses it!' she said. She added that her own mother 'would love to see this' and gave me a very contented smile. That was great. I felt emboldened now and thought of my previous travelling companion. I said goodbye to this lady and her children and disembarked from the train.

In my next prayer asked God that if I was meant to give another miraculous medal to my first companion and her brother, it would be easy, with no obstacles and I would catch up with them naturally and without hurry at the ticket aisles. This happened without any obstacles and without much ado, I bumped into the woman and again thanked her for supplementing the cost of my meal on the train. I gave her two blessed medals and advised her to google St Catherine Labouré for further information on the miraculous medal. 'Oh,' she said 'my granny would love this...' She smiled and seemed grateful for the medals. Now I can see why we need to be modern-day apostles of the Good News, its mammy or granny who have the devotions but perhaps not the young adults and the young parents if these interactions are anything to go by!

13th January 2019

'Dear Jesus, thank you for calling me this morning. I know I have to write.'

All the children are back at school and the first week went well. The weather is very mild for the time of year with not much rain.

Following my experiences on the train to Dublin I had a desire to impart with the children in my class the story of St Catherine Labouré and how Our Lady instructed her to form the miraculous medal during an apparition in Rue de Bac, Paris in 1830.

Around this time, I had asked the sixth class children to choose the name of a Saint that had particular meaning for them for their upcoming

Confirmation. One of the girls picked St Catherine as her Confirmation name. It had been a tradition in her family for the girls to pick the name of Catherine for their Confirmation.

Making Miraculous Medals in the classroom

As part of the lesson about the origins of the Miraculous Medal, I showed a little Vimeo clip of the story of St Catherine to the class. The pupil in question said that this was St Catherine her granny had picked for her Confirmation name! (There is also a St Catherine of Siena and St Catherine of Alexandria).The children were very interested in the story and this prompted me further to find out if we could make the miraculous medal. I looked up and found a suitable art and craft activity for the children.[22] We made A4 size miraculous medals with the children in school using strong tinfoil, felt material and A4 paper templates of the miraculous medal back and front and a blunt pencil.

The children went home with their Miraculous medals on Thursday evening. One child came up to me the following day and declared 'O Miss, I had an accident with my Miraculous Medal. My little cousin was in the house and she scrunched up my medal into a ball!' 'Oh I said and what did you do then?' She said 'I took it off her, flattened it out and smoothed it out straight away. Guess what Miss, all the edges were all crumpled and messy, but Our Lady was perfectly smooth….!' I remember feeling a great sense of joy when I heard this. Who knows all the wonderful things Our Lady can accomplish through our 'Yes' to God. I also thought about how wonderfully our Lord is communicating with this young girl. Sometime later, after a visit from our new diocesan examiner, Teresa, who chatted to the children about her experience in Medjugorje, the same child came up to me asked me to look up pictures of Our Lady in Medjugorje!

A Saint for our times - Luisa Piccarreta

Yesterday, I returned two books to a very devout Catholic friend of mine. We spoke about the Divine Will as dictated by Jesus to Luisa Piccaretta. She is recognised as a Servant of God by the Catholic Church. I received a wonderful prayer from them, a Beautiful Prevenient Act Prayer by T.M. Fahy which I am prompted to write here.

'O God, my Father,

I invite the Divine Will to reign in me today just as It does in Heaven; as it did in Jesus and Mary when They were upon the earth. I want all my thoughts, words, and actions to be done in and by the Divine Will, animated and directed by the Divine Will.

I want everything that is done through my humanity to be done in the ambience of Eternity. I want all that I do to fulfil the purpose of Creation, and to realize the ideal that You, Heavenly Father had in creating the human race.I want all my acts to multiply to the infinite, to penetrate everywhere, to embrace all eternity.

I want all my acts today to be adored by the Angels because of being filled with the life of God Himself! I want all my acts in the Divine Will to reproduce the life of Jesus. As my acts begins, I want them to form the Conception and Birth of Jesus; as my acts are carried out, I want them to form the hidden and public lives of Jesus; as my acts conclude, I want them to form the Death and Resurrection of Jesus.

I want my acts of this day to spill over into the Heavenly regions, showering the Angels and Saints with new joys, new glories and new beatitudes; and I call all the Angels and Saints to join me today in all that I do. I want all my acts to effectively impetrate the Reign of the Divine Will on earth as it is in Heaven.

My God, I want all my acts today to enrapture You, bring You ecstasies of new and ever-increasing joys.

I want all my acts today in the Divine Will to repair all human acts, past, present and future to make them all Divine Acts for your honour and glory, my Father.

I want all my acts today to penetrate every creature ever created past, present, and future / to bring to you, Father an 'I love You, adore You, praise You and thank You from every thought, word and deed ever done by them, or ever will be done by them.

I love You my God, divinely, infinitely, eternally. I love You for as long as You have been God and for as long as You will be God, which is Eternity itself, with Your own Will, in the name of all generations past, present, and future. I love You my God, my Father, the Author of my life! Amen.' [23]

Every morning I start my day with an abbreviated form of this prayer:

'Eternal Father,

I offer up all my thoughts, words, joys, sufferings, deeds, prayers and inclinations this day for the Eternal Father in the Divine Will, through Jesus, Mary, St Joseph and all the angels and saints in heaven, in the name of all souls past, present and future. Amen.'

31st January 2019

'Dear Jesus, I am here to write for you.'

Jesus

'Write about my mercy and God's justice.'

Just as the Tuam Mother and Baby Home scandal captures the news again, no realisation is present in the minds of those who voted 'Yes' in the Abortion referendum that they have, in a premeditated way, sanctioned the slaughtering of innocents.

In a quote from the Irish Catholic November 30th 2017, 'Patrick', one of the former residents of the Tuam Mother and Baby home, says: *'They now want to offer abortion as a solution to 'unwanted children' – sure that isn't me' he said.*

'If abortion was legal back in the day, I probably wouldn't be here. The people that were born in Tuam – sure we'd be the first ones aborted...' [24]

God will not be fooled. He knows what's in people's hearts.

'He that is without sin among you, let him cast the first stone at her .....and they who heard it, being convicted by their own conscience, went out one by one.....and Jesus was left alone, and the woman standing in the midst.' **John 8:7-9.**[1]

'Thank you Lord for calling me.'

10th February 2019

First Divine Will Prayer Meeting

Since I wrote last, I have been to my first Divine Will prayer meeting in Galway. I found it very inspiring and am currently studying the works of Servant of God, Luisa Piccarreta. I am reading a wonderful introduction to the Work and its connection with other great Saints by Daniel S. O'Connor called 'The Crown and Completion of All Sanctity.' www.dsdoconnor.com.[25] It is a great read from, in my humble opinion, a very genuine and gifted author, for any person who wishes to understand more about the 'Gift of Living in the Divine Will'. *'The Servant of God, Luisa Piccarreta was a 19th and 20th-century Italian mystic whose revelations from Jesus, encompassing thousands of pages of material, give an amazing insight into a new gift of sanctity for the Church, namely, the Gift of Living in the Divine Will. In this book, you will find an introduction to just what this "Gift" entails, an explanation of how to receive this Gift yourself, and a theological defence of its orthodoxy a perfectly compatible with Catholic faith and morals.'* (p.1 The Crown and Completion of All Sanctity).[26]

17th February 2019

Overhearing a 'divorce' meeting in hotel

'Dear Jesus,

Thank you for getting me up out of bed. May God bless anything I write.'

Last week I went to our local hotel with my youngest child for a little treat – a scone and a cup of hot chocolate. We found a nice seat for ourselves in the lounge area and waited for our order and chatted. He likes to read and so he took out his book and read while we waited for our order. Meanwhile, I noticed, there were four people next to us engaged intently in conversation to our right. At first, I didn't pass any remarks as I was very much enjoying the company of my son. They are only small children for a while, so these years are very precious!

Nevertheless, the conversation going on to my right got my attention and I am not one for listening to other peoples' conversations! There was an attractive blonde-haired lady in her mid to late thirties sitting next to her father and two lawyers. They were discussing her upcoming divorce and about 'settlement' issues - who would get what in terms of property and land, etc. after the divorce. I noticed the legal pair were very slick and well-practised and convincing with their advice about same. The whole party were very intent in talking out everything and were not at all ashamed about how loud they were and that other people could hear them. One of the legal people mentioned the upcoming referendum in May.

This referendum is about conditions necessary before a couple can get a divorce. It refers to the period of estrangement, which is currently four out of five years being reduced to two out of three years. The woman in the group, who was wishing to divorce her husband was sitting forward, listening to the advice of the legal team as if they were gods. All four of them were oblivious to the other diners in the lounge. Though I didn't hear all parts of the conversation, nor did I want to, I heard the woman say something about her child crying to her in relation to the pending separation. She was blaming her husband about this. This immediately struck a familiar chord with me. It was at this point I moved my son and I to a different part of the lounge to finish our meal.

There are no winners in legal battles such as this. I understand this from being a child in such a situation. I also know how the future is likely to play out for that family if that divorce goes ahead. This is how the tape goes – the couple are still relatively young and attractive, there will be a battle of wills and legal teams on both sides to settle the financial aspects of the divorce, this will be followed by a battle for custody rights, usually, the mother gets full custody with the father getting visitations rights.

In the years ahead, the couple are 'now free' to meet other people and enter into new relationships. Often these will not last or the ones that do will have other problems, perhaps not dissimilar to the problems the first marriage encountered due to their own faults and failings. Meanwhile, the children of the marital union will bear the brunt of the emotional rollercoaster and shame associated with the breakup of the family unit. They will absorb a lot of the hurt because they won't know who to turn to. The parents will defend their own positions and they may even talk about 'the way things are' to their children, but something has happened to the children's minds and hearts. A part of their hearts has been shut down. They are no longer carefree and grow up quickly to become adult children.

Hence the reason for brokenness to take hold in later life as discussed above. Divorces are sometimes described as being amicable but the hurt of rejection is still there until hardness of heart sets in. How can it be friendly if the love that was there in the first place is being cut off permanently? The cracks appear when 'love is withdrawn' by one spouse more than the other, at first. God IS love so anything that takes away love is not from God, it is due to sin. This leads to an eventual withdrawal of love on the part of the other spouse too, because love has to be reciprocated in order for the love bond to be complete.

When Jesus was asked what the greatest commandment of the Law was by one of the Pharisees, He replied: *'Love the Lord your God with all your heart and with all your soul and with all your mind. This is the first and greatest commandment. And the second is like it: Love your neighbour as yourself. All the Law and the prophets hang on these two commandments.'* **Matthew 22:34-40.**[1] The word neighbour means 'everyone' and if this is true, then most certainly, it is a commandment to couples to love one another just as Jesus loves 'us' despite all our faults and failings. If Jesus commands us to love our neighbour and *'love your enemies'* **Luke 6:27-31**[1] then He commands us all the more to love our spouse because love conquers everything, *' Love is patient, love is kind. It does not envy, it does not boast; it is not proud. It does not dishonour others; it is not self-seeking; it is not easily angered; it keeps no record of wrongs. Love does not delight in evil but rejoices* *with the truth. It always protects, always trusts, always hopes, always perseveres.'* **1 Corinthians 13:4-7**[1]

How many marriages could be saved if every couple held this message in their hearts? If we love God, the ultimate source and object of our love, won't He be all the more receptive to our pleas to help us love others in times of trial. Our efforts to love will produce fruit hundred-fold and will be passed down through the generations. Love is what binds families together and provides a secure home for our children. Love gives them strong roots for life and enables them to 'persevere' in all the trials of life, and there is no family without trials.

'Thank you, Jesus. I can do nothing without You.'

1st March 2019

The power of prayer in numbers

'Thank you, Jesus for prompting me to write this morning.'

I am writing about the power of prayer in numbers. My cousin Emily is sick with cancer at the moment. She lives in Slovenia with her family. Over the past few months, I have been in contact with her mother. Before Christmas I got word that Emily had cancer and that she was undergoing some new drug trials to try to eliminate it. One evening I felt a strong prompting to ring my aunt to ask how she was doing. (We had not been in contact for some years.) She was delighted I phoned and was telling me she was making good progress with the treatment and that a friend of hers was talking about going to Medjugorje in June. Of course, having had a great experience there, I was singing the praises of the place and highly recommended that she go and that a lot of people experience healing over there. I told her about my own healing experience as well. She was very interested in hearing about it. So we concluded the call on a very positive note and she asked me to pray for Emily.

A number of weeks later I got a call from my aunt. She was very distressed and crying. She informed me that Emily was dying and only had days to live. The treatment had not been successful. Emily is only 41 and she has a husband and young family. Her mother asked me to pray for her as she was not at all at peace. I said, of course, I would and that I would ask our adoration prayer group to pray for her as well. She said all the immediate family were coming over to be with her in the coming days. She said she would be in touch. I asked the prayer group on the Whatsapp group chat (fifty one members) to pray for Emily and in particular if they could pray the Divine

Mercy Chaplet. Jesus said to St Faustina, *'Pray as much as you can for the dying. By your entreaties (that is insistent prayers) obtain for them trust in my Mercy because they have most need of trust and have it the least. Be assured that the grace of eternal salvation for certain souls in their final moment depends upon your prayer.'* – **Diary of St Faustina 1777.**[27]

Some people replied and said they would and I have no doubt those that didn't reply were praying for her as well. Having heard nothing from my aunt, I contacted her two weeks after my last conversation with her in which Emily was close to death. I got a text which said "Hi Shirley, good to know you are praying for Emily. She's had a week of radiotherapy and has another week to go. She's very tired and weak but is in fairly good spirits. Please keep praying because I believe it's making a difference. Say thanks to your prayer group from us all. I'll be in touch. Take care." Please God Emily will continue to be at peace and make good progress. Thank you God for everything.

5ᵗʰ March 2019

'Dear Jesus, thank you for getting me up to write.'

My story about Emily continues. My husband and I were in Knock at the weekend. It was bustling with people. My first stop was the Chapel of Reconciliation.

I realise fully, for some time now, that the sacrament of Confession is crucial to our staying close to God and attempting, with His grace, to operate all our daily activities in His Divine Will. How easy it is to sin and for our own human will to get in the way of God's grace! I hasten to add that before my conversion, I wasn't really even fully aware of what constituted a sin. I do remember being given a Penny Catechism when I was a child, but my mother was probably uncomfortable with reading through and explaining the content to me. Or perhaps I wasn't listening carefully to her! I knew the obvious things to avoid like stealing and murder but was ignorant of the equally serious sins of omission of kindness, avoidance of acts of justice, slander, impure thoughts etc. which slowly degrade the mind and the soul and which harden the heart. If only people knew how unburdened, they will feel by going to Confession with a firm intention to try not to sin again, and 'accepting' that God forgives us.

The 'accepting' part sometimes needs to be worked on especially for more serious sins, but God is true to his word as this quote from Isaiah 1:18 states: "Come now, let us settle the matter", says the Lord. "Though your sins are like scarlet, I will make them white as snow. Though they are red like crimson, I will make them white as wool." So niggling thoughts that we are not forgiven are not from God and they prevent us from living more fully in His Divine Will. Here is another quote. First letter of St. John **1 John 1:9** *'If we confess our sins, he is faithful and just and will forgive us our sins and purify us from all unrighteousness.'* [1] Or this uplifting quote from St Paul to the Corinthians - *'Therefore, if anyone is in Christ, the new creation has come: The old has gone, the new is here!'* **2 Corinthians 5:17**.[1]

After confession, while Eamon was in the Apparition Chapel, I popped into one of the local souvenir shops 'The Crown of the Rose' just opposite the Parish church. While in there, the only other customer in the shop at the time happened to be talking to the shopkeeper about St Peregrine, who is the patron saint of those suffering from cancer, AIDS or other serious illnesses.[28]

To be honest, I had never heard of this saint before, so I was interested in learning more. After his conversion to Catholicism St Peregrine devoted his life to the poor and the sick. He developed a cancerous sore on his leg and the night before an amputation operation was scheduled, he spent the night in prayer before a crucifix in the hospital chapel. He dreamt at one point there that Christ came down for the cross and healed his leg. When he woke up he and his doctors, discovered that he was completely cured! Countless numbers of people have been cured of cancer through his miraculous intercession. (ourcatholicprayers.com). The lady in the shop said that St Peregrine's medal is supposed to give great relief if the sufferer holds it in their hand and places it on the affected area. As it turned out, my aunt had been putting St Peregrine's oil on Emily every day. So she was delighted to get a St Peregrine's medal which I bought in the shop, got blessed and subsequently sent on to her with a Divine Mercy prayer leaflet.

For anyone who hasn't been to Knock here is a brief story about what happened there in 1879 which has made Knock a place of renown and Pilgrimage ever since.

Story of Knock

On the evening of the 21st August 1879, Our Lady appeared at the gable of the church with St Joseph, St John the Evangelist holding a book of the Gospels and the Lamb on a plain altar. 'Some saw angels hovering around the lamb. The witnesses watched and prayed for over two hours in the pouring rain and while the wind from the south was driving against the gable, it remained perfectly dry. Our Lady was dressed in white robes with a cloak fastened at the neck. Her eyes and hands were raised in prayer toward heaven.' (www.knockshrine.ie). A unique aspect of the story surrounding the apparition was the completion on the same day of one hundred masses offered for the Holy Souls by Archdeacon Cavanagh, Parish Priest of Knock at the time.

One and a half million pilgrims visit Knock every year. There are now five churches altogether. These include the Apparition church, the Parish church, the Basilica, the Blessed Sacrament Chapel and the Chapel of Reconciliation. There is also a religious book shop, a caravan and camping park, a hotel, a museum (hidden away to the back of the religious book shop behind the Chapel of Reconciliation but not to be missed!) and beautiful gardens around the Shrine. Recently a mystic Priest Fr Michel Rodrigue was given the words that St John the Evangelist was preaching during that apparition! At the time of the apparition in 1879, no words could be heard, but it was evident that St John was preaching something from the book he was holding.[29]

20th March 2019

'Thank you Jesus for prompting me to write. I think of you every day and try to carry you in my heart in all situations.'

I have regular contact with someone who is suffering from depression at the moment and I've heard it called the 'black dog'. This seems to be a very apt description. I surrender that soul to Jesus during the most difficult communications with this person. May God's Will be done in this situation. Thank you God for my continued strength and the fire of my love for you.

Studying the Divine Will writings of Luisa Piccarreta

On Saturday last, I attended my third 'Divine Will' prayer meeting in the Franciscan Abbey in Galway. It was truly superb. We are just finished studying volume six of Luisa Piccarreta's writings of her experiences with Jesus and heaven. If a person is well disposed, it truly touches the core of their being. All other reading/studies I have undergone through Divine intervention have culminated in this great work of Jesus through Luisa (thirty six volumes). The Lord to date has guided me in his own inimitable way to the writings of Padre Pio, St Teresa of Calcutta, Pope John Paul II, Maria Valtorta, St Faustina, St Thérèse of Lisieux and now Luisa Piccarreta.

I remember how very amazed but also reassured I was when I read Daniel O'Connor's book, The Crown and the Completion of All Sanctity which gives a great introduction to the writings of Luisa Piccarreta. It was as if all the jigsaw pieces were being put together in the right order. All Jesus needed was for me to say 'yes.' All Jesus needs is for all of us to say 'yes.' When you do, who knows the wonderful work He has in store for you to do! He needs us all in these troubled times of persecution for the Church. As Paul says in his letter to the **Philippians 1:6**, *'And so I am sure that God, who began this good work in you will carry it on until it is finished on the Day of Christ Jesus.'* [1]

'Thank You Jesus, we love You and adore You and praise You Jesus.'

30ᵗʰ March 2019

The Gift of Living in the Divine Will

'Dear Jesus, this day finds me struggling with thoughts of what you want of me, so I'm just going to let you take over.'

I am studying the works of Luisa Piccarreta and realise how far short human beings fall of walking in God's ways. Who or what is the Divine Will? The Divine Will is God's Will. As the Our Father prayer states: …Thy Kingdom come, Thy Will be done on earth as it is in heaven. So in as far as possible we must pray and do all our acts in the Divine Will with the help of Jesus and Mary and all the angels and saints in heaven, in the name of all souls past, present and future for the glory of God. We are ultimately trying to save souls and in the process hopefully shortening our own time in Purgatory. The Gift of Living in the Divine Will is a higher level of spirituality. It is assumed that anyone embarking on this journey has already attained a certain degree of understanding of spirituality up to this point.

The putting aside of the human will for good is the most difficult thing we need to do. We have to let God direct our lives completely and operate in the Divine Will twenty four hours a day, not just dip in and out of it as our human will dictates. This is especially difficult for people (i.e. most of us!) who would like to have absolute control over everything in their lives! In order to live in the Divine Will, of necessity, we must clothe ourselves in humility. God cannot operate in our lives without this humility and appreciation of our 'nothingness.' After all, mortally speaking, we come from nothing and we return to nothing. As the quote **Genesis 3:19** states: *'In the sweat of thy face shalt thou eat bread, till thou return into the ground; for out of it wast thou taken: for dust thou art and unto dust thou shalt return.'* [1]

31st March 2019

The eyes are the windows of the soul

Jesus has just illuminated my conscience on a question I've always asked myself. Why am I looking out of and operating from this body that I (my soul) occupy? Why am I not looking out through the eyes of Pat, or Jean or Thomas? As I was asking this question, it became clear to me that my soul is in essence enclosed or incarcerated in this body or mortal coil. It seemed to me that it would be a very happy soul when it is released from this body at the point of death assuming I have persevered in trying to live a good and holy life and succeeded in overcoming the self.

This realisation gave new meaning to a quote I have often heard "the eyes are the windows of the soul". How apt, the soul, as it were, is looking out of the window of the eyes. Like a bird which flies into a room and perches on a window ledge waiting sometimes patiently, sometimes impatiently to be set free. It is no wonder as we age, that it is harder to stay on the path to holiness as our bodily sufferings increase if we haven't opened our hearts to Jesus in early life. It dawned on me that it is so important to do the Will of God in our lives while we have the health and energy to do so – to keep persevering and not succumb to our human will.

On a separate note, an uncle of my husband passed away during the week, as did my cousin Emily on the same night, (may they rest in peace). My father-in-law had a dream during that night about his brother having died and that funeral arrangements were being made. The next morning they were informed that he had died. This gave my father-in-law great hope for the after-life because he said that he never dreams or at least never remembers his dreams, let alone dream very specifically that his brother had died and that funeral arrangements were being made. The Lord is truly wonderful how he lets Himself be known to us. All He needs is a 'window' of opportunity!

26th April 2019

Visiting my Mother

How quickly time is moving on. Thank you for the beautiful Easter Jesus. It was wonderful participating in the Easter ceremonies and spending more relaxed time with my family. I am truly blessed. Yesterday I visited my mother with three of my children. It is not a very long journey, about one and three-quarter hours, but the roads are bad with lots of bends. I am so glad I made an effort to visit as it is always for me a mixture of sadness, gladness and fear about how the visit will go. The children were very well behaved as they are getting older now. My mother and I spoke with each other in the kitchen after dinner as the children watched TV in the other room…

The past few days, I had been feeling the old familiar sadness and heaviness of heart that used to plague me whenever I thought about my birth family. I thought I had been healed of this hurt and brokenness. I now realise that Jesus was 'just reminding me' of how I felt before I was healed because He wants to use me for something else that is part of the Divine plan if only I say 'Yes' to Him. After all, He has done for me how can I refuse?

These feelings reminded me that there are so many hurt children out there with no one to help them because society is accepting the culture of divorce as the norm…

I felt the sadness sweep over me when I was talking with my mother in the kitchen. I cried and spoke about the hurt caused by the break-up and explained to her how she and Dad had no idea of what it was like because they were so caught up in their own pain. I said how I felt God was calling me to do something to help those hurt people in the form of writings or a testimony talking about my healing journey with the help of Jesus Christ, my Lord and Saviour.

Thank God that mum is being drawn to our faith again and was actually in agreement with my thoughts about helping others. During the conversation with my mother, I could see a robin fluttering energetically outside the window. Another bird, a member of the tit family, was tapping his beak frantically on the window of the shed. I remember the last time we had a heartfelt conversation like this the same thing happened - a robin made himself noticeable to me by hopping and fluttering outside the window...

Prayer

'I thank you Lord every day for my health and healing and may my family and all broken families be healed of the trauma of divorce and separation.'

15th May 2019

I woke early this morning and felt prompted to write by Jesus. I write here sitting on the chaise longue outside our bedroom. The weather is beautiful, sunny and dry. Apparently, this weather poses more of a threat for forest fires than in the later summer months as the gorse and dry un-decomposed vegetation from last year can easily set fire at this time of year. I have so much to write. Jesus and Our Lady are working powerfully in my life every day. Thank God that I notice. I am so anxious to let others know the healing power of God's Love.

It was no accident that I bumped into the holy lady, I wrote about earlier, who helped me on my road to healing that day when she stopped me in the car park. It was on Divine Mercy Sunday after confessions and she was sitting at the front of the church. She looked radiant with the Holy Spirit. She indicated for me to come and sit with her. God was using her again to help me. I had been wondering why in prayer I had not been really aware of Our Lady's presence but always tended to think of Jesus and pray to Jesus at a deeper level, with the exception of when I did the novena – thirty three days to morning glory by Fr Michael Gaitley. She pointed out to me that this was because I had had a difficult relationship with my mother on account of the separation and divorce. The relationship between my mother and I had not been as strong, reliable, and loving as it could have been… Thank God for this beautiful prayer she gave me:

Prayer for help to love a family member who has hurt you

'Dear Mother Mary, please help me to love my (mother/ father/brother/sister) like you love her/him. Also help them to love me as you love Jesus. I give this now to you Mother Mary and to your son Jesus as you know how to love better than anyone on this earth.'

Our Lady has made herself known to me a crucial times such as in the classroom when I prayed to her shortly before my parents split up and also when she was constantly prompting me to go to Medjugorje in the year before I actually went. And now Mother Mary is calling me again this time through my young teenage son who asked me a number of times to go to the Youth festival in Medjugorje. Praise God!

I love this quote from **Ezekiel 36:26, NIV** *'I will give you a new heart and put a new spirit in you; I will remove from you your heart of stone and give you a heart of flesh.'* [1] This was God's promise to the Israelites and the Lord keeps his promises…

4th June 2019

'Dear Mother Mary, Jesus and St Joseph - the protector of families, it has been a difficult past few weeks. I feel a great prompting to write. Let me explain, one of my children is sitting the Leaving Certificate tomorrow

and the other teenager announced he was going on holiday with his friends next week and will not be coming with us on our family holiday. This is the first time he will not be coming with us for our summer vacation, so that will be a big change for us as a family. As his mother, I am concerned for his well-being and of course all the temptations he will face on his personal holiday. It is so difficult to keep children in the faith these days. There are so many distractions, even for parents. The mobile phones truly are a mixed blessing. This is the period where our older two children are beginning to pull away from us. Of course, we have to accept this, but I find sometimes their coarse language in front of the younger children is bothersome. Heaven protect them...'

Enthronement to Divine Mercy – A blessing for the home

We are very blessed in our community to have a new Holy priest Fr Jerald, from Bangalore, in India, We invited him to our house to enthrone our family to the Divine Mercy at the end of May.[30] It was a lovely well-prepared service where we prayed the prayers of Consecration of our family to the Divine Mercy and the Deliverance prayer. These are very powerful protection prayers. Fr Jerald also blessed all the rooms in our house with holy water and incense. Fr Jerald brought us a beautiful image of the Sacred Heart of Jesus and a framed picture of the original Divine Mercy image. The original image was instructed by Jesus to St Faustina in Vilnius.   We felt very blessed after his visit, thanks be to God.

2nd July 2019

'Dear Jesus, Thank you, thank you, thank you for my life with all its ups and downs. I only want to serve you.'

Jesus

'Tell the world about my mercy. It is infinite and unfathomable. Listen not to your own thoughts. It is I who write this. I will give you all you need. Love me every day and I will do my work through you. I will take over. If only everyone would offer up all their joys and sufferings every second to soothe me. Help me to save the world. You are doing it slowly. I will give you wings to reach out to save more souls for me. Do not worry about what you lack. I will make up for it. Keep calling on me in your everyday chores. Watch for me in your neighbour. I have entrusted you with much. I know you feel unworthy and without the mental capacity to achieve what I want. Never fear I will make up for what you lack. Do not be afraid. You are with me and I with you. In you and in me

we are totally immersed in one another. Love me as I love you. Love my mother. She loves you dearly and will help you to cling to me. I will operate in you every day of your life if you let me. Do not fear for your family. I will look after them in the best way possible for their salvation. There will be no obstacles to the work I am giving you. Do not fear; I love you.'

'Thank you Jesus. Help me always to do your Will.'

11th July 2019

Carmel Revisited

'Dear Jesus, thank you for calling me to write.'

Just after returning from our family holidays I was bringing our daughter to her summer job in Loughrea and had the intention of calling into the Carmelite Abbey in Loughrea where I had the children enrolled in the brown scapular last summer. My reason for calling was that we had lost a couple of our brown scapulars and needed replacements, so I called to the Carmelite Abbey office where I had purchased them before. The lady behind the desk checked with one of the priests who came down to reception rather sheepishly after fifteen minutes to tell me they had run out. I was told that the best place to get them was in St Joseph's Monastery in Mount Carmel, Loughrea where the scapulars are actually made.

Well I was very surprised, firstly that they had run out but also I'd never heard of the Carmelite monastery and I was very curious to see this place. While I followed the directions, I had a great feeling that the Holy Spirit was directing my journey. I called into reception and rang the bell. I was greeted by a lovely smiling nun. Her name was Cynthia and she is one of three nuns from the Philippines who were welcomed to St Joseph's in 2004. We had a brief exchange of words and I explained how I was studying the writings of Luisa Piccarreta. Her eyes opened wide as I told her and I was saying how it was lovely to find someone who was interested in discussing such a subject. She said 'I bet there aren't too many friends you have with whom you could interact about that subject.' I said 'no there aren't!'. We discussed other matters briefly and she asked me to call back another time which I will do. I went away feeling it was more than a number of brown scapulars I had received! Praise the Lord!

Excerpt from the website of St Joseph's Carmelite Monastery

'The great Jubilee Year 2000 was over, but vocations to our Carmel were scarcer than ever, and eight sisters *had died since 1980. We needed new vocations, but we knew that in Ireland and England, what had once been a steady flow had dwindled to almost a trickle. We prayed and reflected and talked about this among ourselves and many different ideas surfaced. Finally, Mother Elias Black decided to do something concrete before it was too late. We were aware that many Carmels were actually closing. With the full backing of the community, Mother Elias appealed to the Assoc. of Carmelite nuns in the Philippines for help, i.e. to send us three or four fully professed Carmelite nuns, so that our Carmel would not have to close. After a lot of negotiations and indeed dogged persistence, our wish was granted and on August 6th, 2004, three lovely, fully professed Carmelite nuns from three different Carmels in the Philippines, walked into our monastery, to stay with us forever. It was an unforgettable experience as Srs. Mary Concepcion, Rose-Alice and Cynthia took their place among us, in the simplest possible way, adding smiling faces to this great gift of themselves. June 2005 and they are still with us, which gives us real hope for the future. Meanwhile, we hope to get many good Irish vocations. The God of surprises must be trusted if one is to experience the exceptional surprises only He can give.'* Source – www.loughreacarmel. com.[31]

13th July 2019

'Dear Jesus,

I am here for you. Help me to live inside your Will. I flee from my own will, which causes me to be introspective and selfish. Use me as an instrument of your love. Help me to discern right from wrong. Let me always walk in your footsteps. Praise be Jesus, praise be His holy name, praise be His holy birth, praise be the Mother of God, most sweet virgins of virgins. Blessed be all acts done in his holy name. Thank you, Jesus. Help me always to respond to your call.'

Chapter Five

Further Recollections on Medjugorje

11th August 2019

'Dear Jesus, Mary, St Joseph and all the angels and saints in heaven, thank you so much for the beautiful pilgrimage to Medjugorje which my son and I were privileged to be part of. Please help me to write a fitting account of the highlights of this pilgrimage to help others know the heavenly blessings which come from this holy place.'

Recalling my Pilgrimage to Medjugorje – 30th July – 6th August 2019

A group of young people and three mothers set off for the Youth Festival in Medjugorje from Athenry led by Athenry Youth Group Leader Keith Kelly and Castlebar Youth Group Leader Fr Shane O'Sullivan. We travelled by bus to Dublin airport on Monday night into Tuesday morning 30th July 2019. The flight from Dublin airport to Dubrovnik was pleasant and we arrived there late in the morning to a beautiful sunny day. A further three-hour journey to Medjugorje by bus would complete the journey. Or so we thought...

We were given a history of the apparitions occurring in Medjugorje since 1981 by our tour Guide. She told us of the three checkpoints we would have to go through on the Croatian/ Bosnian border before we reached Medjugorje. Part of this process involved handing over our passports to be examined by the local police. We were a little bit nervous parting with them! We passed through the first two checkpoints with relative ease. Then we were stopped at the third checkpoint. We seemed to be parked there for a long time, at least an hour. Luckily, we were chatting with friends or getting to know new people on the bus, so it passed the time.

Our Guide meanwhile was outside the bus talking with the authorities. She returned to the bus and then proceeded to tell us that there was a problem with the papers of the bus driver, so another bus had to be organised to take us for the remaining journey to Medjugorje. We waited a further hour before the replacement bus arrived. Fortunately, the Bosnian authorities ensured that our luggage was transferred to the new bus. Apparently, there had been talk of transferring the luggage separately to Medjugorje..! This coupled with the fact that our passports were also with the authorities created a little bit of worry. But one of our passengers courageously said that there would be great graces from this trip because of the difficulties we were experiencing…She turned out to be right! Thanks be to God!

From the outset, my son loved everything about the trip: the camaraderie with the other young people, the daily excursions, the outdoor Holy Mass and the testimonies and teachings of the group leaders. He is looking forward to going again, God willing.

Recalling My Experience of Our Lady's Apparition to Mirjana 2nd August 2019

The morning of the apparition of Our Lady to Mirjana, we had to be up at 4.30 a.m. Well we had a choice actually. We could be up at 4.30 if we wanted to be at the White Cross (which is at the top of the mountain – Cross Mountain), for the rosary with Ivan (Ivan Dragicevic is one of the six children Our Lady first appeared to in Medjugorje in 1981)[32] before the apparition at the blue cross with Mirjana, or we had to rise at 5.30 to be on time and in our places for Mirjana's apparition at the Blue Cross only.

I opted to get up at 4.30 am and bring my son

with me to go to Cross Mountain to pray the rosary. This way I figured we would be walking down the mountain to the Blue Cross for the apparition instead of walking up to it later when the crowds would be worse.

So after much cajoling of my young son, to put it mildly, we left the hotel with bread and water in our bags and met our Group leader at Our Lady's statue in the grounds of St James' Church. After about half an hour, we headed off with our Group Leader and a priest by taxis to the base of the mountain. From there we start to climb on foot. The climb is not too difficult, that is, not too steep, but you do have to watch your footing on jagged rocks. The priests of the various groups led the rosary on the way up. It took about an hour and a half to reach the top Cross Mountain (where the White Cross is). This is where Ivan prayed the rosary. It was lovely and I was so looking forward to Our Lady's apparition at the Blue Cross, which was going to happen at 9.30 a.m. We made our way back down to the Blue Cross and were there at about 7.15 am. By this stage, my son had moved on through the crowds to find the rest of his group who were coming up later.

There is a wall along the road in front of the Blue Cross and a lot of people had begun to congregate among the rocks and the dirt tracks near the cross which is surrounded by a walled seating area enclosing a well-adorned statue of Our Lady (flowers and rosary beads). It's quite amazing how many people can sandwich themselves into a relatively small area. I felt Our Lady was calling me to get a close as possible and I also had the feeling she would let me know when I was finally to stop.

There were quite a few obstacles on the way to my final halting-place. First of all, a very cross Italian lady said to me, "You can't go any further!" when it was clear there were spaces for me to stop further up. Next, I passed a rocky shelf on which another lady was hovering on some unstable rocks. She urged me not to go any further, saying "You'll hurt yourself!" I soldiered on regardless.' It would be still another two hours before Our Lady would appear. Then after another bit of weaving throughout the crowd without further fuss, I could see the Blue Cross in plain view.

Finally, I eyed the destination where I sensed Our Lady wanted me to stop. It was under a small tree and I would be able to see the Blue Cross clearly while not being in the final enclosure, described above. The final obstacle was in the form of a large framed Italian man. When he saw me trying to get in around him where there was clearly some space in front of him, he said squarely to me "No!" and with a corresponding aggressive gesture of his hands made it clear I would not pass him. There was a man standing next to him and I prayed for a gap to form between the two men so that I could slip in between them and make my final few steps forward to arrive at my final destination – the small overhanging tree.

My prayers were answered and a gap appeared. Without further ado I slipped through and perched on a rock under the tree. I didn't look back at the displeasure on the man's face, but I heard a few disapproving grunts coming from him. It didn't matter; I was where Our Lady wanted me to be. In fact, I smiled to myself as I remembered the story of Zacchaeus as he hid in the tree searching for a glimpse of Jesus. Now all I has to do was wait. Meanwhile, I let another person, who had eyed a place she wanted to get to, past me. I'm pretty sure the Italian man who had said 'no' to me saw this happen as it was right in front of him.

So the wait was on as we all prayed the rosary together. From time to time loud noises could be heard. This I presumed was people being released from their hurts, bondages, demons, etc. I could not see Mirjana, but it was very clear when Our Lady arrived because the praying stopped and people had their cameras ready to capture the wonderful privilege of being present for Our Lady's apparition. In front of me, part of the wall was missing from the enclosure. There was a woman standing a couple of feet away from me. She was with a man who was probably her husband.

All of a sudden Our Lady appeared. There was a temporary hush in the crowd as everyone, including me, held up their cameras in order to capture the moment. (Anyone who has seen YouTube videos of Our Lady's apparitions to Mirjana will know that even if people do not actually see Our Lady, though some do, they know she is there, by a feeling, or a change of atmosphere, or a change in the light, or by Mirjana's change of appearance during Our Lady's presence.) At the moment the apparition started the woman referred to above collapsed on the ground in a seated position. She was releasing a sound that was from deep within her like a wail. She continued wailing for a while and then she became quieter. All the while, the man who was with her had his hand on her shoulder as if to comfort her.

There were other cries or wails from the crowd. To be honest, the ones who emitted a deep guttural sound, (though at this point I could only hear this in the distance), it was my impression that they were releasing demons. My personal experience was that

I was shaking and half crying faintly and expelling breaths from my inner depths. I can't explain it, but I got the sense that souls were being released through me. I have never before had this experience, so I think Our Lady was blessing me in this particular way during this apparition. Everyone there was blessed in some way. Even the stern, large Italian man who wouldn't let me pass, he mumbled "scusé" as I passed him when we were leaving - a softer, more humble demeanour had overcome him. Praise God!

When the apparition was over, people made their way slowly and carefully down the mountain. By this time, it was starting to get hot. Here and there, you could hear people being spiritually released - there were a lot of priests on the mountain and some were occupied giving exorcism blessings on some very fortunate individuals. They are fortunate because they will go home free from bondages or oppressive spirits and renewed in spirit. I witnessed an older woman and a young man being blessed by priests as they released their demons or bondages. I'll never forget the look of pure joy on a young man's face as he almost fell into the arms of his mother after being prayed over and blessed with Holy water by the priest. Thanks be to God!

Over the years Our Lady has communicated five stones which will keep the faithful on the holy path.

Our Lady's 5 stones

In her messages to the visionaries in Medjugorje, Our Lady has given us what she calls '5 stones' 'as a weapon against your goliath'.

The little stones are:

1. Prayer with the heart: The Rosary

2. The Eucharist (Holy Mass)

3. Holy Bible

4. Fasting

5. Monthly confession.

Prayer with the heart : The Rosary

Our Lady has asked persistently at Fatima and Medjugorje that we pray the rosary. She said *'Dear children, Pray! Pray the Rosary every day - that wreath of flowers which, as a mother, directly connects me with your pains, sufferings, desires, and hopes.'* **Our Lady's apparition to Mirjana September 2, 2019)**[33] It is a very powerful prayer against evil and has the power to stop wars. *'In 1945, Hiroshima, Japan, a priest and seven others survived the nuclear bomb that was dropped on Japan and had devastating effects during the Second World War. Even though they lived near* *ground zero, much to scientists' amazement, these survivors were free from all harm caused by radiation even years later. What was different about this group of people compared to other nearby victims? It was their devotion to the Rosary. They prayed the Rosary together daily.'* (**www.howtopraytherosaryeveryday. com**)[34]

It only takes fifteen minutes of a person's day. It is within reach of most people to pray and meditate on the mysteries of the Rosary every day to receive God's protection for themselves, their families and to offer it up for Our Lady's intentions. Whoever honours Our Lord's mother sincerely in this way is very pleasing to Him.

She also said, *'Every family must pray family prayers and read the Bible.'* (**February 14, 1985**)[35]

The Eucharist

'The Church obliges the faithful to take part in the Divine Liturgy on Sundays and feast days and prepared by the Sacrament of Reconciliation, to receive the Eucharist at least once a year, if possible during the Easter season. But the Church strongly encourages the faithful to receive the Holy Eucharist on Sundays and feast days, or more often still, even daily.' (**CCC 1389 Catechism of the Catholic Church CTS Definitive**

& Complete Edition prefaced by an apostolic letter written by Pope John Paul II).[36]

Our Lady has said in her messages:

'Mass is the greatest prayer of God. You will never be able to understand its greatness. That is why you must be perfect and humble at Mass, and you should prepare yourselves for it.' **(Our Lady of Medjugorje 1983)**[37]

The third Commandment also requires us to keep holy the Sabbath, *'For in six days the Lord made heaven and earth, the sea and all that is in them and rested the seventh day; therefore the Lord blessed the Sabbath day and hallowed it.'* **Exodus 20:11**[1]

The Holy Bible

The Bible is the word of God. It keeps us connected with the truth. A good place to start if you are not sure where to begin is the Gospel of Matthew chapters 5, 6 and 7. (www.biblestudytools.com) The core message of Jesus's teachings are in these chapters.

The Ten Commandments given to Moses by God are listed in the book of Exodus, chapter 20:1-17.

There are other ways to read the bible. There some beautiful examples on forums.catholic.com[38] of testimonies from people who have opened their bibles at random to see a scripture and meditate on it to help them with a question or problem they might have. Penny from Canada writes: 'I have at times, in prayer and conversation with God, asked him to 'give' me a scripture in His kindness, to read and meditate on. Many times things would happen during the week that reminded me of the scripture I got earlier, and it created another opportunity to talk with God. It felt like He was part of my day, my week, and was there caring for me...'

Fasting

Fr Slavko Barbaric OFM, a Holy priest who grew up near Medjugorje, wrote a book about fasting.[39] Very simply he describes fasting as a means to grow in holiness. In the introduction to his book, Sister Betwy also explains the different forms of fasting in practical terms.

She writes: *'we are all called to fast, even the elderly, the sick and the young. However, not all are called to fast in the same way. We should seek God, ask His direction and then follow the impulses we sense coming from Him. Some persons may be urged to fast on bread and water (the 'best fast according to Mary), others may be called to give up smoking, alcohol, or television. Others may follow the Church's regulation for fasting on Ash Wednesday and Good Friday which states that 'a person is permitted to eat one full meal, as well as two smaller meals that together are not equal to a full meal.'*

Confession

When I first went to confession after many years of not availing of this sacrament, I used to marvel at how quickly some people were coming out of the confession booth. I think it's because they have made confession a regular habit, so their sins haven't had a chance to build up. A person who hasn't been to confession for a long time will naturally be nervous about the experience and will probably (a) be unsure what constitutes a sin - check this link for clarification (www.beginningcatholic.com/catholic-examination-of-conscience)[40] and (b) use the opportunity to have a short counselling session with the priest.

By the way, priests are really well trained nowadays to hear confession and they are very understanding. There is no sin they have not heard about in the confessional! It's not like years ago when you would be quivering with fear in the confessional waiting for absolution and the priest might have a very serious or strict demeanour! But remember the priest is there standing in for Jesus so when he absolves you of your sin which is sincerely confessed, that is Jesus forgiving you! How great is that?! Then you pray whatever penance the priest gives you and you walk back into your life as light as a feather. Your soul has just been spring cleaned. Padre Pio used to recommend that people attend confession as often as possible. Even if they were the same annoying miserable little sins, he called it a dusting of the cupboards!

18th August 2019

Other Reflections about Medjugorje

In contrast to the beautiful weather we had in Medjugorje, today is a very wet heavy day today. It has been a very unsettled summer in Ireland with lots of monsoon type showers and muggy heat. I know Jesus wants me to write, but I can't help but feel a bit dispirited. I thought I would be giving a testimony of my own faith journey in Medjugorje, but it turned out not to be the right time. I know I have to accept God's timing for this, but it's hard not to be impatient because I feel ready to give it. The week had been full of testimonies from different people for the youth. Some were lovely testimonies of how people found their faith along their pilgrim journeys; others were more dramatic testimonies of how their lives were turned around from a life of drugs to a strong faith-filled life with a calling to give back to society.

A lovely girl called Angel on the trip was an invaluable source of support. She is truly a very holy person with great wisdom for her years. We chatted about 'God's timing' for moving forward in our lives within His Will. The fact that I don't feel peace about the matter perhaps means He wants me still to do something in this regard, but not at this time.

Prayer

'Dear Jesus, Mary, St Joseph and all the angels and saints in heaven, please help me to be patient and to be sensitive to the promptings of the Holy Spirit.'

God helps those who help themselves

To continue on about my story of Our Lady's apparition to Mirjana above, I was very happy I made an effort (helped by Our Lady) to climb higher and closer to the site of the apparition on the 2nd August. God truly does help those who help themselves. Our priest Fr Jerald recently conveyed this in a well-known story recently, called 'God Will Save Me' – It goes like this: 'A terrible storm came into a town and local officials sent out an emergency warning that the riverbanks would soon overflow and flood the nearby homes. They ordered everyone in the town to evacuate immediately.

A faithful Christian man heard the warning and decided to stay, saying to himself, "I will trust God and if I am in danger, then God will send a divine miracle to save me." The neighbours came by his house and said to him, "We're leaving and there is room for you in our car, please come with us!" But the man declined. "I have faith that God will save me." As the man stood on his porch watching the water rise up the steps, a man in a canoe paddled by and called to him, "Hurry and come into my canoe, the waters are rising quickly!" But the man again said, "No thanks, God will save me." The floodwaters rose higher pouring water into his living room and the man had to retreat to the second floor. A police motorboat came by and saw him at the window. 'We will come up and rescue you!' they shouted. But the man refused, waving them off saying, 'Use your time to save someone else! I have faith that God will save me!' The floodwaters rose higher and higher and the man had to climb up to his rooftop. A helicopter spotted him and dropped a rope ladder. A rescue officer came down the ladder and pleaded with the man, 'Grab my hand and I will pull you up!' But the man STILL refused, folding his arms tightly to his body. 'No thank you! God will save me!'

Shortly after, the house broke up and the floodwaters swept the man away and he drowned.

When in Heaven, the man stood before God and asked, 'I put all of my faith in You. Why didn't You come and save me?'

And God said, 'Son, I sent you a warning. I sent you a car. I sent you a canoe. I sent you a motorboat. I sent you a helicopter. What more were you looking for?'[41]

7th September 2019

'Dear Jesus,

Thank you for calling me.

The children are all back to school and college now and after a week into it, the daily routine of work and study is now settling in.'

6th November 2019

'Thank you God for everything and thank you Jesus for inspiring me to write this morning. I feel a great sense of gratitude. I'm teaching in a new school and feel that already, the change, has re-motivated me not only in work, but also in other areas of my life too. A change is as good as a rest, they say!'

15th December 2019

'Dear Jesus,

Thank you for calling me to write.'

It is coming up to the most beautiful time of the year – the birth of our Lord and Saviour Jesus Christ. This calls to mind the beautiful Anticipation prayer which begins on St Andrew the Apostle's feast day, November 30th and is recited fifteen times a day until Christmas Day. It is as follows: *'Hail and blessed be the hour and the moment in which the Son of God was born of the most pure virgin Mary at midnight in Bethlehem in piercing cold. In that hour vouchsafe, I beseech thee, Oh my God, to hear my prayer and grant my desires (here mention your request) through the merits of our Saviour Jesus Christ and of his blessed mother. Amen.'* [42]

1st March 2020

'Dear Jesus,

Thank you for inviting me to write today. It is the 5th day of lent. Thank you for the gift of the short vacation for my husband and I to the home place of your Servant of God, Luisa Piccarreta. May all my actions be carried out in the Divine Will, through

Jesus, Mary, St Joseph and all the angels and saints in heaven in the names of all souls, past, present and future for the glory of the Eternal Father. It has been a long time since I have responded or felt called to write. You know the crosses I have to carry and I thank you so much that you have answered my prayers and for all the prayers of those close to me. It is so true that you never test your followers beyond their limits.'

As Jesus says: – *'Peace is what I leave you, it is my own peace that I give you. I do not give it as the world does. Do not be worried and upset; do not be afraid.'* **John 14:27.**[1]

At this time, the novel coronavirus is spreading across the world, with two cases reported in Ireland in recent days. There are also very regular storms affecting Ireland over the past month. Ireland has seen the return of fifteen pro-life TDs to the Dáil after the recent general election, while a significant number of the more strident pro-choice advocates lost their seats including the Minister for Children.[43]

Solemnity of the Annunciation of the Lord - 25th March 2020

From the 13th March onwards the daily Mass could no longer be celebrated for the public because of the spread of Coronavirus which means that Catholics are unable to receive the Holy Communion, The Eucharist, sacramentally. This was actually predicted in the Old Testament of the Bible in the book of **Daniel 12:11** – *'From the time that the daily sacrifice is abolished and the abomination that causes desolation is set up, there will be 1,290 days.'* [1]

Today on the solemnity of the Annunciation of the Lord, there was the Consecration of Ireland to the Immaculate Heart of Mary by Archbishop Eamon Martin from Armagh Cathedral at twelve noon delivered by Webcam.

Interestingly in 1984 Pope John Paul II consecrated Russia to the Immaculate Heart of Mary and not long afterwards came the breakdown of Communism culminating in the demolition of the Berlin Wall in 1989.[44]

6th April 2020

'Thank you Jesus for calling me to write.'

It has been an unparalleled few weeks since our country's decision to close schools and colleges in a bid to curb the spread of COVID-19 – the novel Coronavirus. Ireland is now on lockdown with even more stringent restrictions put in place preventing the movements of old people (the highest mortality rate so far of all the Coronavirus deaths) outside their homes and gardens.

These are unprecedented times in the land of Saints and Scholars, a heretofore strongly Catholic country.

In the last 5 years, the majority of voters in the Republic of Ireland voted for gay marriage,[45] legalised abortion for any reason up to twelve weeks,[46] the removal of the offence of blasphemy out of the constitution and the reduction in the period of estrangement to make it easier for couples to dissolve their marital union.[47]

How times have changed since the first men orbited the moon…

Chapter Six

Conclusion

On Christmas Eve December 1968 the astronauts William Anders, James Lovell and Frank Borman, were the first humans to travel to and orbit the moon on the spacecraft Apollo 8. Anders was amazed when after their fourth orbit around the moon he caught sight of the 'Earthrise' seen below, which the astronauts had not spotted on the previous three orbits. They had been instructed by NASA to 'say something appropriate, on the success of their mission. In their broadcast, they read Chapter 1, verses 1-10 of the book of Genesis thus honouring God for his wonderful creation.

'We are now approaching lunar sunrise, and for all the people back on Earth, the crew of Apollo 8 has a message that we would like to send to you.'

William Anders

'In the beginning God created the heaven and the earth. And the earth was without form, and void; and darkness was upon the face of the deep. And the Spirit of God moved upon the face of the waters. And God said, Let there be light: and there was light.

And God saw the light, that it was good: and God divided the light from the darkness.' [7]

James Lovell

'And God called the light Day, and the darkness he called Night. And the evening and the morning were the first day. And God said, Let there be a firmament in the midst of the waters, and let it divide the waters from the waters. And God made the firmament, and divided the waters which were under the firmament from the waters which were above the firmament: and it was so. And God called the firmament Heaven. And the evening and the morning were the second day.'

Frank Borman

'And God said, Let the waters under the heaven be gathered together unto one place, and let the dry land appear: and it was so. And God called the dry land Earth; and the gathering together of the waters called the Seas: and God saw that it was good.

And from the crew of Apollo 8, we close with good night, good luck, a Merry Christmas – and God bless all of you, all of you on the good Earth.'[7][48]

James Lovell would later go on to captain the ill-fated Apollo 13 which never got to the moon due to a fault in the design of the oxygen tanks which when stirred caused an explosion on the service module. *'The crew overcame limited fuel and electrical power, a failing air filter system that led to increasing levels of carbon dioxide and the threat of a tropical storm blowing the capsule far off course from its expected landing destination.*

For Jerry Woodfill, who served as NASA spacecraft warning system engineer for Apollo 13, the spacecraft's successful return has shaped more than his professional career. The event has resonated within him and shaped his view of God's role in fashioning events. Without divine intervention, he says, the crew and Johnson Space Center's mission control team could not have overcome obstacles and brought the astronauts home safely.' (**Houston Chronicle April 20, 2018**)[49]

If brilliant scientists and astronauts can be humbled before God, doesn't this also apply to the rest of us? We are all called to trust in Our Lord in times of need. Clearly, as shown here, science and faith can work in harmony. God gives the scientists their gifts and by return, when solutions go outside the realm of their understanding, faith, hope and love remain. And the greatest of these is love! God loves His creation and He wants us to love Him back and to trust in Him.

So if you are searching for answers and in need of healing, open your heart to Jesus and He will show you the way. As Jesus himself said to His apostles - '*I am the way, the truth, and the life, no one comes to the Father except by me.*' **John 14:6.**[1] We are all called to be modern-day apostles for Christ. Each one of us has a gift to be used for the good of all.

Apollo 8 view of earthrise over the moon ... Christmas Eve, 1968. Photograph: Bill Anders/AFP/Getty Images

Please Review

Dear Reader,

If you were blessed in some way by this book, would you kindly post a short review of *Jesus the Healer* on Amazon or book seller site you purchased from. Your feedback will make all the difference to getting the word out about this book.

To leave a review on Amazon, type in the book title and go to the book page. Please scroll to the bottom of the page to where it says 'Write a Review' and then submit your review.

Thank you in advance for your kindness.

Shirley

Endnotes

1. New International Version Bible, Biblica; and the Catholic Good News Bible, Collins, the Bible societies.

2. The Irish Labour Market and the Great Recession - https://www.esri.ie/system/files?file=media/file-uploads/2015-07/JACB201234.pdf

3. Pope John Paul II visit to Ireland - https://www.irishtimes.com/news/ireland/irish-news/pope-john-paul-ii-s-1979-irish-visit-1.3589702#&gid=1&pid=1

4. Padre Pio: *The Scent of Roses - Irish Miracles and Cures* by Colm Keane, Veritas.

5. Franco Zeffirelli's *Jesus of Nazareth* by William Barclay, 1977.

6. Shrine of Padre Pio - www.padrepio.ie

7. Relic of Padre Pio - Manfredonia, 12-3-1971 Archbishop Valentino Vailati.

8. *Vicka....Her story* by Finbar O'Leary, Dufour Editions

9. The Statue of the Risen Christ - Medjugorje https://medjugorjeca.org/pilgrimage-itinerary/statue-of-the-risen-christ/

10. YouTube clip - Flashes of light in St. James's Church, Medjugorje https://youtu.be/WLb9av_1fxo

11. The Penny Catechism - http://www.catholictreasury.info/catechism/cat18.php

12. The Irish Catholic Catechism for Adults, Irish Episcopal Conference, Veritas, 2014

13. Divine Mercy in *My Soul Diary of St Maria Faustina Kowalska* Marian Press 2016

14. St Teresa of Avila prayers - https://www.catholicity.com/prayer/prayer-of-saint-teresa-of-avila.html

15. *33 Days to Morning Glory - A Do It Yourself Retreat in preparation for Marian Consecration.* Fr Michael E. Gaitley MIC.

16. Society of African Mission (SMA) - Our Deceased https://defunts.smainternational.info/en/necrologe/2233-le-pere-john-michael-monahan

17. St Michael the Archangel Prayer - https://saintmichaelcc.org/prayer-to-st-michael-the-archangel

18. Explanation of the Sabbatine privilege of the Carmelite order - https://ocarm.org/en/content/ocarm/explanation-sabbatine-privilege

19. Page 42, '*33 days to Morning Glory*'

20. Page 33 Lucia speaks - *The Message of Fatima* by John Hauf & Marie Ostermann, 2007.

21. The history of the Miraculous Medal - www.catholicism.org/miraculous-medal.

22. Making miraculous medals with children - www.catholicicing.com/miraculous-medal-craft-for-catholic-kids/

23. *A Beautiful Prevenient Act* by T.M. Fahy - http://www.comingofthekingdom.org/luisateachings/downloadable-prayers/a-beautiful-prevenient-act/

24. Irish Catholic newspaper - Tuam Mother and Baby Home -https://www.irishcatholic.com/not-name-tuam-survivors-reject-calls-repeal-pro-life-law/

25. *The Crown of Sanctity: On the revelations of Jesus to Luisa Piccarreta* by Daniel O'Connor https://www.goodreads.com/book/show/44234107-the-crown-of-sanctity.

26. https://www.goodreads.com/book/show/25084581-the-crown-and-completion-of-all-sanctity

27. Page 629, 1777, Diary of St Faustina.

28. Prayers to St Peregrine - https://www.ourcatholicprayers.com/prayers-to-st-peregrine.html

29. Fr Michel Rodrigue - Our Lady of Knock : https://www.countdowntothekingdom.com/fr-michel-rodrigue-message-from-our-lady-of-knock/

30. Enthronement to Divine Mercy - https://www.thedivinemercy.org/chj/prayers/familyoffering

31. 'Our sisters from the Philippines' - History of St Joseph's Carmelite Monastery, Loughrea https://www.loughreacarmel.com/our-history/

32. 'My Heart will Triumph' - Mirjana Soldo 2016 https://www.amazon.co.uk/Heart-Will-Triumph-Mirjana-Soldo/dp/0997890606

33. Our Lady's 5 stones - Rosary - https://medjugorjelive.org/2019/09/02/mirjana-apparition/

34. Rosary protection at Horoshima - http://www.how-to-pray-the-rosary-everyday.com/military-victories-through-the-rosary.html#japan

35. Every family must pray family prayers and read the bible.':https://www.webmedjugorje.com/index. php/messages-xm-of-our-lady-xm/weekly-messages-xm-from-medjugorje-xm-2/516-14021985-weekly-message-february-14-1985

36. *The Eucharist: CCC 1389 - Catechism of the Catholic Church* CTS Definitive & Complete Edition prefaced by apostolic letter written by Pope John Paul II.

37. 'Mass is the greatest prayer of God...'Our Lady of Medjugorje, 1983 - https://www.medjugorje. org/livingmessages.htm

38. The Holy bible picking a scripture at random - www.forums.catholic.com

39. *'Fasting'* by Father Slavko Barbaric - https://www. amazon.co.uk/Fasting-Fr-Slavko-Barbaric-ebook/dp/B007W4SY82

40. Confession - examination of conscience (www. beginningcatholic.com/catholic-examination-of-conscience)

41. 'God will save me.' - http://epistle.us/inspiration/ godwillsaveme.html

42. Christmas Anticipation Prayer - https://www. ewtn.com/catholicism/devotions/christmas-anticipation-prayer-343

43. https://gript.ie/many-of-the-most-strident-voices-for-abortion-have-lost-seats-in-election-2020/

44. Pope John Paul II consecration of Russia to the Immaculate Heart of Mary - https://www.marian.org/fatima/about/russia.php

45. Same Sex Marriage in Ireland - https://en.wikipedia.org/wiki/Same-sex_marriage_in_the_Republic_of_Ireland

46. Abortion in Ireland - https://www.irishtimes.com/news/politics/abortion-referendum

47. Divorce and Blasphemy in Ireland - https://en.wikipedia.org/wiki/Thirty-eighth_Amendment_of_the_Constitution_of_Ireland

48. God's creation described by Apollo 8 Astronauts -https://en.wikipedia.org/wiki/Apollo_8_Genesis_reading

49. Divine Intervention - Jerry Woodfill on Apollo 13https://www.houstonchronicle.com/life/houston-belief/article/NASA-engineer-says-God-intervened-in-Apollo-13-12852254.php